BASEBALL'S ART OF HITTING

BASEBALL'S ART OF HITTING

George Sullivan

Illustrated with photographs and diagrams

DODD, MEAD & COMPANY

New York

FRONTISPIECE: *Tony Oliva was the best natural hitter of recent years.*

To Tim, for much help

ACKNOWLEDGMENTS

The author is grateful to the many people who assisted him by providing source material and photographs for use in this book. Special thanks are offered the following: Harry Walker, St. Louis Cardinals; John Redding, National Baseball Library, National Hall of Fame and Museum; Seymour Siwoff, Elias Sports Bureau; Frank McMenamin, Hillerich & Bradsby; Frank Torre, Adirondack; Gary Wagner, Wagner-International Photos; Herb Field, Herb Field Studios; Joe Reichler, Office of the Baseball Commissioner; Bob Fishel, Vice-President, New York Yankees; Hal Middlesworth, Public Relations Director, Detroit Tigers; John Wright, Aluminum Company of America; Dan Bishop, Monsanto; Buck Peden, Chicago White Sox; Bob Hope, Atlanta Braves; Larry Shenk, Philadelphia Phillies; Larry Chiasson, Montreal Expos; Art Santo Domingo, San Francisco Giants; Bob Wirz, Kansas City Royals; Dino Lucarelli, Cleveland Indians; Wayne Chandler, Houston Astros; Tom Mee, Minnesota Twins; Irv Grossman, San Diego Padres; Fred Claire, Los Angeles Dodgers; Bill Crowley, Boston Red Sox.

CONTENTS

Cincinnati Red Stockings inspect their bat trophy.

GOOD-BYE TO THE .300 HITTER

While there is evidence of professional baseball being played as early as 1866, the Cincinnati Red Stockings of 1869 are regarded as the game's first professional team. That year the Red Stockings played 65 games and didn't lose one. The only blot on their record was a 17–17 tie with the Troy (New York) Haymakers.

Midway in the season, after the team had made an all-conquering swing through the East, the Red Stockings returned to Cincinnati where they received a joyous welcome. City fathers, to show their appreciation, decided to present the team an award, something unusual.

It should be a bat, they agreed, but not just an ordinary bat. This would be the biggest bat ever made—twenty-seven feet in length, nineteen inches around at the barrel end. The trophy was hoisted aboard a wagon and carted out onto the field where the Red Stockings were engaged in a "Welcome Home" game.

A bat was an appropriate symbol for the game in those days. The Red Stockings, although aided by rules which restricted the pitcher's windup, hit the ball like a team possessed. Some scores that season were:

Red Stockings, 65; Omaha, 1
Red Stockings, 103; Cincinnati Buckeyes, 8

Red Stockings, 76; San Francisco, 5 (called at the end of five innings)

As anyone who has read a box score recently knows, those days have gone the way of gas lighting and high-button shoes. If a team were to win 65 games in 66 tries today, and the fans and city officials wanted to demonstrate their appreciation with an award, you can be sure that it wouldn't be a bat. A bronzed rosin bag would be more appropriate. Or one of those small carts that bear relief pitchers in from the bullpen.

It is a matter of fact that the bat is no longer the symbol of baseball. The pitcher is—and baseball is the poorer for it.

Hitting is action. A hit—a single, double, or triple—puts a man on base and starts the chain of events that leads to runs crossing the plate. This is what makes baseball exciting. Home runs are exciting, too, but less so. After the ball is struck and the hitter has rounded the bases and disappeared into the dugout, there's a letdown. The home run, in a way, mutes the vitality of the game. There's a big bang, then it's over.

In the seasons that followed the glory years of the Red Stockings, the restrictions on pitching were gradually lifted, and by 1885 the pitcher was in control of the game. The pendulum was then allowed to swing the other way, and so it went, with the rulesmakers favoring the batter for a time, then giving the advantage back to the pitcher.

The year 1920 marked one such turning point. That was the year that the "lively" ball was introduced, and trick pitches like the spitball and emery ball were made illegal. Babe Ruth responded to the rule changes by hitting 54 home runs that year. The highest number he hit in any previous season was 29.

Every team's offense improved. Whereas teams had churned out only seven or eight runs per game with the "dead" ball, they were now able to score nine to ten runs a game. When the total reached eleven runs per game in 1930, the owners took some of the bounce out of the ball, but it was still regarded as frisky.

In the years that followed, baseball's offense went into a gradual decline. By 1963, the runs per game total was down to less than eight. In 1968, which has been called "The Year of the Pitcher," the figure hit a modern low when fewer than seven runs per game were scored.

Baseball officials were worried. To reverse the trend, they did two things: they lowered the pitcher's mound and they made the strike zone smaller. These modifications worked to the benefit of the hitters, but only for two years. Pitchers learned to adjust and by 1971 the runs-per-game totals were going down again. The amount of scoring in 1972 was about the same as it was in the old dead-ball days.

Why is this? What's happened to baseball's offense? Part of the answer can be found in this piece of doggerel.

> See the ball before you stride;
> Make sure it's not in or outside.
> If it happens to be low
> Hold your bat and let it go.
> But if it happens to be any place around
> Take a good swing and hit it downtown.

These were the words that Walt Williams of the Chicago White Sox used to say to himself as he went to the plate. What makes them worth noting here is that Williams, who was traded to Cleveland in 1972, was, at 5-foot-6, the smallest man in baseball. Yet Williams felt that his size, or lack of it, was no deterrent toward his becoming a home run hitter. Like everyone else in modern baseball, Williams wanted "to hit the ball downtown."

"The home run pays off in today's society," says Dixie Walker, hitting coach of the Los Angeles Dodgers. "Young players are determined to knock the ball out of the lot. The result is, we have more home runs today than ever before—and fewer guys who can hit .300.

"To smash homers, you have to pull the ball. Well, there's no way you're going to pull a slider on the outside corner."

Walker points out that today's hitters, in an effort

Hitting is frequently an all-or-nothing matter. Carl Yastrzemski demonstrates.

to achieve distance, are using lightweight bats. This enables them to whip the bat around with lightning speed. "I'm not suggesting that hitters go back to using the long, heavy bats that were used years ago," says Walker. "But the fact is that light bats are more conducive to power and less conducive to a good average.

"The man with the heavy bat would merely try to meet the outside pitch. He would take any kind of hit he could get. Today, the kids with light bats will gamble on belting an outside pitch out of sight."

Walker believes that one day new standards will apply in baseball. He sees an end to .300 as a mark of hitting excellence. One day, he says, .250 will be regarded as being perfectly respectable.

The urge to hit home runs can be traced to baseball's earliest days. Henry Chadwick, in his booklet "The Art of Batting," published in 1885, was critical of batsmen who "go for a style of batting which pleases the crowd, though it proves costly in the long run to the success of the team." He also noted that home run hitters were, "as a class, the easiest victims to strategic pitching."

Chadwick blamed the press for the situation, at least in part. "The reporters," he said, "see nothing worthy of special praise aside from 'two-baggers,'

Roger Connor was one of baseball's first sluggers. He hit 136 home runs from 1880 to 1897.

'three-baggers,' and home runs. The custom of singling out for publication the names of batsmen who make these hits and runs is responsible for their striving more for this sort of glory than for the best interests of the club they represent."

Today, Chadwick would undoubtedly point the finger of blame at the owners. The biggest salaries go to the players who hit the most home runs.

As hitters have become less knowledgeable, less willing to practice the subtleties of the art, pitchers have been getting stronger and more sophisticated. The best example of this is the slider, a pitch that has come to represent a major part of the hitting problem.

Whitlow Wyatt, who pitched for the old Brooklyn Dodgers in the early 1940s, is credited with "inventing" the pitch. He is said to have come upon it by accident while "fooling around" during an exhibition game. He soon found that it solved the basic problem a pitcher has in 2-0, 3-1, and 3-2 situations of "getting the ball over but getting something on it."

A kind of a cross between the fastball and the curve, the slider zoomed in popularity after World War II and it is in widespread use today. The pitch looks like a fastball until it nears the batter, whereupon it veers to the right or left and, thus, out of the batter's swing-arc. This is in contrast to the curveball, which breaks down and away from the hitter.

The slider might have been regarded with the same general lack of interest as the palmball, forkball, and other secondary pitches, except that hitters helped to make the slider effective. Yes, *hitters* did. They did it by virtue of their home run swings. The slider's delayed break, extremely difficult for the hitter to perceive, was made to order for striking out the make-or-break hitter. It is almost as if the hitters were conspiring in their own ruin.

The spitter is another pitch that hitters are facing with greater frequency, although its use hasn't yet come to equal the slider's. The spitter used to be a "waste" pitch, used chiefly when the count was 0-2 or 1-2, but hitters now see it in critical moments.

Sure, the spitter is illegal, but umpires are very lax in enforcing the rule that prohibits the pitch. Clubs condone having their pitchers use the spitter; coaches teach it. Every pitcher has tried it. Umpires have little wish to try to reverse the trend.

Some pitchers have become famous—or notorious—for their use of the spitball. Gaylord Perry of the Cleveland Indians is one. Perry was on the mound recently against the Yankees. A fly ball went to New Yorker center-fielder Bobby Murcer. As Murcer trotted in, he made a point of wetting the index and middle fingers of his right hand, then rubbing the ball with them. As he flipped the ball to Perry at the mound, the grinning Murcer said, "Just getting it ready for you, Gaylord."

Yankees' star reliever Sparky Lyle awaits the call to action.

Hank Aaron called the more frequent use of relief pitchers "the biggest reason" that higher batting averages were hard to obtain. "You don't get to see a guy three or four times in a game any more," Aaron declared. "I don't mean a guy weakens in the late innings necessarily, but you get a better chance to hit him because you've seen him.

Now you just get a good idea about a guy and he's gone."

The relief pitcher used to be a pitcher that the manager kept in the bullpen because he wasn't good enough to be a starter. His status was about that of the utility infielder or backup catcher. But a dependable reliever is now held in almost the same esteem as a 20-game winner. Tug McGraw of the New York Mets and Sparky Lyle of the New York Yankees were each paid about $70,000 in 1973 as relief pitchers. No wonder it has become a highly regarded specialty.

Leonard Koppett, who has written knowledgeably and incisively in *The Sporting News* about the decline in baseball's offense, has stated that the "main factor" is the poor quality of umpiring. He says that the strike zone has "fuzzy" dimensions. "Umpires call many strikes on pitches that are not really in the strike zone," says Koppett. Because the essence of good hitting is to have an accurate idea of the strike zone, the effect of careless umpiring is, to use a word of Koppett's, "devastating."

Koppett has also noted that the gloves used today have had a detrimental effect on batting averages. The original idea of the glove was to protect the hand from stinging pain or injury, but little by little the concept changed. Today's gloves are

Fielders' gloves of the early 1900s were not much bigger than hand-size.

16

easily twice the size of those in use a couple of generations ago, and maybe they're three times as big. Just as important, they are fitted with big ball traps that help to transform the most fumble-fingered of fielders into a slick ballhawk. Indeed, they do about everything but make the throw.

It's not just gloves that have gotten bigger. Stadiums have, too, and this has hurt hitting. Fifty or sixty years ago, when a baseball club put up a park to play in, the idea was to build it close to public transportation, to trolley car terminals and, later, to subway stations. Then came the automobile. Nowadays people drive to the park and, thus, stadiums can be built in suburban areas, where there is plenty of room to spread out.

None of the new stadiums has anything to compare with the left-field wall in Boston's Fenway Park, only 315 feet from home plate. So many hits carom off it, pitchers refer to it as "the Green Monster." In Forbes Field in Pittsburgh, the right-field fence was only 302 feet from the plate. The Polo Grounds in New York was beer and skittles for the pull hitter. The distance down the right-field line was 280 feet, and down the left-field line only 250 feet.

Ballparks with dimensions like these have gone —or are going—the way of good penmanship and neat house painters, to be replaced by monster stadiums with acres of space for fielders to patrol. Not only are there fewer home runs, but fewer dou-bles and triples. And, because pitchers can afford to be a little bit less careful, fewer walks, too.

Synthetic turf, which has been installed in about one-third of the major league stadiums, being harder, firmer, and more resilient than grass and dirt, is supposed to be a great boon for hitters. Balls that would normally be scooped up by infielders skip right through. This is true, however, only on those synthetic fields which have retained the skinned portion—dirt—between bases. A ground ball that comes ripping off the synthetic surface and takes a bounce on the skinned portion of the infield is a problem for the infielder. The Pittsburgh Pirates have an infield of this type and some observers say that it is one reason why the Pirate batting averages have climbed so in recent years.

But in parks where the *entire* infield is synthetic (except the mound and areas around the bases), it's a much different story. At first, hitters were able to rifle the ball right past the infielders. But the infielders learned to adjust by playing deeper. On a field that's completely synthetic, such as the one found at the new Riverfront Stadium in Cincinnati, the second baseman stations himself practically in short right field when a left-handed hitter is at bat. The shortshop plays almost as deep. "It's impossible to get a ground ball past them," laments Pete Rose of the Reds, "unless you hit up the middle."

Baseball's defense has also been strengthened by

Candlestick Park is typical of the new stadiums. It's 410 feet from the plate to center field, 335 feet down each of the foul lines.

shifting infielders into the area, or areas, where the batter is expected to hit the ball. When left-handed power hitters such as Billy Williams of the Cubs or Willie McCovey of the Giants came to the plate, they usually found three infielders playing on the right-field side of second base, and the left fielder in left center. When right-handed pull hitters such as Nate Colbert of the Padres or Hank Aaron came up, the fielders shifted in the other direction.

Why doesn't the hitter thwart the shift by hitting to the "wrong" side? He can't—or won't. A left-handed hitter who has been pulling the ball to the right side since his Little League days isn't going to learn another hitting style overnight. It requires months of practice. Because it takes a long time, and because he has a fear that such tinkering might ruin his swing for all time, he doesn't try. It's much easier to go for all or nothing.

Finally, there's the schedule. It involves a mix of 162 night games, day games, twi-night games, and doubleheaders over a period of 178 days on one coast or the other and most of the big cities in between. The travel and boredom quickly tires hitters, weakens them. Seldom do players eat at

AstroTurf goes down in Busch Stadium.

19

the same time or sleep at the same time on two consecutive days. Of course, pitchers are subject to the same rigors. But a starting pitcher works only one day out of every four. The other days he can rest.

There's much that could be done to reverse the trend, to beef up baseball. It could be as simple as reducing the size of the strike zone. Shaving an inch or so off the size of the plate would have the same effect.

Fielders' gloves could be made smaller. The rules regarding illegal pitches—the spitter, that is— could be strictly enforced. They could liven up the ball again, although this suggestion might only work to increase the prevalence of the do-or-die swinger.

The Sporting News has said that the answer to the problem is to move back the pitcher's mound. "The pitching distance has been 60-feet, 6 inches since 1893," the publication notes. Players were smaller in stature then. The fact that they are bigger and stronger today has benefited only the pitchers, who are able to throw a great deal harder.

Owners could stop paying home run hitters all that money. The highest salaries should go to the intelligent, artful batter, to the man who has taken the time and effort to learn his trade.

One thing baseball officials did do in an effort to put more punch into the game was install the designated hitter rule. It permitted a manager to use a pinch-batter, a tenth player, actually, in place of the pitcher. The rule went into effect in 1973 in the American League.

Early evaluations showed the effect of the rule to be less than revolutionary. *The New York Times* presented statistics that demonstrated, to quote the paper, "how surprisingly little difference designated hitters have made."

The rules have been revised countless times in the past century, so as to favor either the pitcher or the hitter. They should be again. Fans want more hitting, more action. Why not give it to them?

GRIP, STANCE, AND SWING

In tennis, Ping-Pong, and other racket sports, the moving ball is struck by a flat surface which is very large in relation to the size of the ball. In golf, the striking surface is much smaller, but the ball is standing still. The hockey stick offers a long flat blade with which to strike the sliding puck.

In baseball it's different. The hitting instrument is a long, slim cylinder. Because it is, there is almost no margin of error. Contact has to be made on the center line of the bat barrel in order for the hit to be an effective one, that is, not a ground ball or a harmless fly.

Add to this the fact that the ball is not merely moving, it is *rocketing* toward the plate. A fastball thrown by a major league pitcher travels at a speed of up to 100 miles per hour, which means that it covers the distance from the pitcher's mound to home plate—60 feet, 6 inches—in less than half a second.

These considerations, combined with the fact that the ball is only 2.87 inches in diameter, make hitting a baseball one of the most difficult tasks in all of sport, if not *the* most difficult. It is no wonder that even the best hitters, those with .300 averages, fail in seven out of every ten attempts.

It is no wonder, too, that hitting has come to be regarded as a science, as an activity worthy of theoretical explanation and experimental investiga-tion. No player ever stops trying to improve his hitting skill. Some part of every day is devoted to the cause.

Hitting begins with the grip. It has to be firm but not overly tight. If the batter tries to strangle the bat, the muscles in his forearm tighten to such a degree that he can't swing properly. Gripping too loosely is just as bad—for obvious reasons. You either grip at the handle end, the bottom hand flush to the knob, or you don't. If you don't, you're said to be choking up on the bat.

There are several advantages and some disadvan-tages to choking up. For one thing, it enables a smaller-than-average man, with less than average strength, to swing a bat that otherwise might be too heavy for him. When you choke up two or three inches on a 34-ounce bat, it feels like a 32-ouncer.

Many batters who choke up do so because the bat feels better balanced. They have greater control and, thus, it's easier for them to make contact. When San Francisco's Garry Maddox produced a steady stream of base hits during 1973 that cata-pulted him into the lead in National League bat-ting, he credited it to choking up on the bat. "Last year I sometimes choked up with two strikes on me," he said. "Now I do it on almost every pitch. My goal is to put the ball in play and avoid striking out." Matty Alou, Sal Bando, and Bert Campanaris are others who have had good results choking up.

Bobby Grich (left) and Sal Bando choke up on the bat.

Ty Cobb, the most successful hitter of all time, as evidenced by the fact that he led the American League in hitting a record twelve times and owns a .367 lifetime average, choked up on the bat. He would wait until the pitch was on him, then push it or slap it. He could hit to any field.

Cobb's grip was unusual because he kept his hands about four inches apart, a style which enabled him to bunt readily. By crouching and waggling his bat, Cobb would often convince the pitcher and the infielders that he was going to bunt, but at the last possible moment he would straighten up and poke the ball into the outfield.

Pull hitters, swing hitters, and sluggers—no matter what term you use—all grip the bat at the very end. This technique enables them to swing freely, swing fully.

A sprinkling of batters use a device that enables them to get a freer than normal swing while choking up on the bat. The device is known as a "bat choke." Made of soft black rubber, the bat choke is the same size as the bat knob, but it has an open center like a doughnut, and thus can be slipped over the bat end and moved along the handle to a spot where it feels comfortable to the batter. Bud Harrelson of the Mets is one advocate of the bat choke.

What the device does is give the batter who chokes up much the same feel as the hitter who grips at the end of the handle. It was Billy Martin, manager of the Detroit Tigers, who got the idea for

Frank Howard (left) and Bill Melton grip at the end.

Ty Cobb had spectacular success with the choke-up grip.

the bat choke. In working with hitters, Martin found that he was able to get them to choke up during practice sessions, but in games they would revert to the habit of sliding their hands to the very bottom of the bat handle. "They didn't feel comfortable unless they had their bottom hand resting against a knob," said Martin. An adjustable knob was the solution.

Like the grip, the batter's stance has to be comfortable. His feet are about shoulder-width apart. His weight is evenly distributed. He bends his knees

Bud Harrelson (below), Bill Russell, and Luis Aparicio are among those who like using the bat choke.

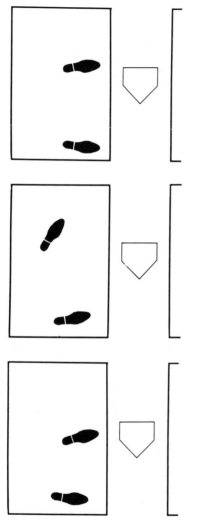

Batting stances—even, open, and closed.

slightly. His shoulders are level.

Some players stand deep in the batter's box, almost touching the back line with the rear foot. Others prefer to be closer to the front line. The general feeling is, however, that there is no great necessity to be closer to the pitcher than you have to, and that if you should put your front foot much ahead of the front edge of the plate, you're putting yourself at a disadvantage.

The stance can be open, closed, or even. An even —or straightaway—stance is one in which both feet are the same distance from the edge of the plate. Few players use this type of a stance, preferring one that is either open or closed. If a batter is not decidedly open or closed, he at least tends toward one or the other.

In taking an open stance, the batter draws his front foot away from the plate and angles it away from the rear foot. (In the case of a right-handed hitter, the front foot is angled toward third base.) Thus, the batter's body is partly turned toward the pitcher.

The advantage of the open stance is that it enables the batter to watch the pitch with greater ease; he doesn't have to peer over his shoulder. It also gives him the opportunity to pull the ball. In fact, it almost forces him to pull. The open stance also makes it easy for the batter to cope with inside pitches. But outside pitches become a problem. Indeed, if the batter's stance is too open, the only

The stance must serve as a solid platform; weight is on the rear foot. This is Lou Piniella.

way he can hit a pitch to the outside is by lunging at it.

The closed stance is just the opposite. The front foot is positioned closer to the plate edge than the rear foot. This enables the batter to cover the entire plate, hitting both inside and outside pitches.

No matter what type of stance he uses, the batter has to get close enough to the plate so as to be able to reach outside pitches. Of all the hitters active during the early 1970s, Frank Robinson stood closer to the plate than anyone. The style enabled Robinson, a right-handed hitter, to pull some pitches he wouldn't be able to pull otherwise. At the same time, he was able to hit to right field with his natural swing. The biggest disadvantage was that pitchers tried to jam him, to curve the ball in on his fists. But Robinson was perceptive enough to recognize when he was about to be jammed and had the quickness to get the bat around in time.

Once the batter has decided on his grip and stance, he can concentrate on the essence of hitting —the swing.

The swing is a move and countermove, a cocking and an uncocking. As the batter awaits the pitch, he concentrates on the ball. He has to be able to feel that he and the pitcher are the only people in the stadium. The idea is to watch the ball from the time it leaves the pitcher's hand all the way to the bat.

As the pitcher begins his windup, the batter shifts his weight to his rear foot and cocks his hips. Getting hip action into the swing is what imparts power. The bat is fairly upright at this stage. The hands are about chest high and positioned above the toes of the rear foot.

As the ball is delivered, the hitter takes a short stride forward, his hips uncock, and he whips the bat into the ball. In the final stage of the swing, the follow-through, the wrists and hands roll over as the bat is swung around. The batter's weight ends up on his front foot.

The swing should be level, although there is some disagreement about this. Ted Williams, for example, recommended a slight upward swing, the type he used. But a swing of this type has to be perfectly timed, since the zone in which contact is made is relatively small when compared to the impact zone of the level swing. Harry Walker, one of the most noted hitting instructors, says that the upward swing is fine if the batter happens to be as gifted as Ted Williams. "But," states Walker, "who is?"

Most managers agree with Walker; they don't want their hitters swinging up. While the level swing is what managers and coaches like to see, they feel there is no great damage done if a hitter chops down on the ball once in awhile. During 1973, Leo Durocher, manager of the Houston Astros, made a deal with his shortstop, Roger Metzger, who had a habit of uppercutting when he swung. Each time Metzger hit a fly ball, evidence of an upward swing, he had to contribute a nickel to a kitty. For every grounder, Durocher put in a dime. The idea, of course, was to get Metzger to hit down.

Why is the level swing best? Because it produces line drives, and line drives are what make for hitting success.

Joe Torre of the St. Louis Cardinals, one of the pre-eminent hitters of the past decade, says that one mistake young players often make is in trying to imitate major league batsmen. "A youngster should develop his own hitting style," says Torre. "He shouldn't copy."

Torre also says that many youngsters slow their development by trying to hit home runs on every pitch, "They get into this habit by watching 'name' players on television or at the park," he says. "A young player should concentrate simply on meeting, on hitting singles. There aren't *that* many Hank Aarons in the Little Leagues."

What other piece of advice does Torre have for young hitters? "When a boy is standing at the plate, he should point his shoulder toward the pitcher, aim it. And as the pitcher winds up, he should step toward him, but still keeping the shoulder pointed in the pitcher's direction. That shoulder should remain facing the pitcher until he begins his swing."

Doing this enables the young player to get the power of his upper body into his swing. Often, says

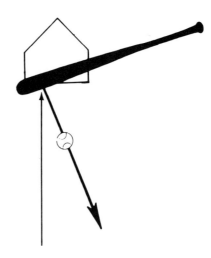

In pull hitting, the bat meets the ball in front of the plate.

Torre, a young player will turn his lead shoulder too quickly, wasting his power. Pointing it, aiming it, helps him to overcome this failing.

While there are countless hitting styles among major league players, virtually all hitters fall into one of two categories. First, there are those who rely on a short, compact swing. They try to meet the ball, to hit line drives. Occasionally they hit home runs, but that is not their chief aim. The second type of hitter is the pull hitter, the free swinger. Pull hitters are home run hitters—or wish they were.

Pete Rose of the Cincinnati Reds best typifies hitters of the first type. "The hitter should try to meet the ball solidly and not overswing," Rose says. "The shorter and more compact the swing, the better the chance of making contact. This is the secret of hitting."

Rose keeps his chin close to his front shoulder as he awaits the pitch. His knees are slightly bent. He takes a hard, level swing, getting the barrel of the bat out in front of the plate. Manny Mota, Joe Torre, and Matty Alou are other hitters of this type. Hank Aaron employed much the same style, at least until 1972, the year he began trying for home runs almost exclusively. Then he became known as a pull hitter.

In order to pull, the hitter must meet the ball before it reaches the plate. Only in this way will the bat be angled so as to send the ball down the line (see diagram). This means that the batter must start his swing earlier, which makes for a longer swing. And the longer the swing, the greater the momentum at the time of impact. This is why a pulled hit is a powerful hit. Combine this with the fact that the distance down either the left-field or right-field line is much shorter than the distance to any of the other fields, and you can understand why pulled hits are often home runs.

When a hitter wants to hit the ball to the "wrong" field—a right-handed hitter hitting to right field, for example—he must swing late in order to meet the ball late. This means that the bat isn't going to develop nearly the momentum it achieves when he

Willie Stargell typifies the modern pull hitter.

29

Stargell unlimbers.

pulls. The result is usually a weak hit.

Willie Stargell of the Pirates is an excellent example of the pull hitter. He is truly a menacing figure at the plate. There's his size for one thing; that alone can intimidate a pitcher. The bat looks like a child's toy in his hands, and he waves it back and forth unceasingly as the pitcher gets ready to throw.

Then suddenly he stops, cocks the bat high, and eyes the pitcher.

Stargell's swing is level, his stride very short. His quick and powerful wrist action snaps the bat around so that it meets the ball well out in front of the plate. His hip action and fully developed follow-through help to explode the ball away.

Concentration—that's what Stargell strives for each time he comes to the plate. "If I don't hit, there's no reason to go away in disgust," he says. "It's only when I give less than 100 per cent in concentration that I go away angry with myself."

Concentration means watching, watching intently as the ball comes off the pitcher's hands and then following it as it comes toward the plate, right until it strikes the bat. Concentration means waiting, too. The longer the batter can wait before he swings, the less likely it is that the pitch will fool him. But waiting also requires quickness, the ability to whip the bat around at the last split second.

While many facets of the hitting swing are in dispute, all hitters agree on one point—that it requires practice and discipline in order to become proficient.

Tony Oliva is an example. Oliva has been called the purest natural hitter in baseball. In 1963, the year he broke in with the Minnesota Twins, he led the league in batting with a .323 average, the first time a rookie had ever won the league batting title. He repeated his feat the next year, hitting .321, and

Concentration is a "must." This is the Tigers' Gates Brown.

did it a third time in 1971, with a .337 average, despite a painful knee injury which required post-season surgery.

Oliva could hit all types of pitching. He could hit to all fields. But he never attributed his success to any inborn talent he might have owned. "I won three batting titles," he said, "and I did it because I concentrated on my work. I studied the pitchers. When I went to bat, I knew exactly what the game situation was and the best thing to do."

If there is any great failing in young hitters, it may be that they don't have the same attitude that Tony Oliva did. Harry Walker thinks this may be true. "Most young players don't practice enough," he says. "Once they make it to the majors, many of them seem satisfied. They don't spend time analyzing their shortcomings and seeking to improve. Too many things distract them. They don't *think* hitting enough."

Joe Torre waits,
sets, swings.

Manny Mota gives bat a pine-tar treatment as he waits to hit.

HITTER vs. PITCHER

When a batter is in the on-deck circle awaiting his turn, he prepares himself carefully, each man having his own elaborate ritual. It may involve swinging a weighted bat, or bats, or his own bat with a doughnut-shaped weight attached. He may, to get a firmer grip, dab powdered resin on the bat handle or wipe it with a pine-tar rag.

Once he gets to the plate, he has groundskeeping chores to perform. Some batters, using their cleats, scuff a shallow hole for the rear foot. Others fill in holes and smooth the dirt.

There's more. As the batter takes his stance, he carefully checks the positioning of his feet. Several practice swings follow. These implant in his mind the groove of his swing, what he wants to achieve when the pitch is released.

But all of these things are really secondary to what's going on in the hitter's mind. Hitting, it is often said, is 50 per cent from the neck up. And it's true.

This doesn't mean, however, that the hitter is thinking about how he is going to swing the bat. Hitting is a reflex action, like putting up your glove to make a catch. You have to limit your thinking to practice sessions. Think about your swing while you're at the plate and the ball will breeze right by you.

What the batter does think about is the pitcher

and his strategy. He knows a great deal about the man he is about to face. He knows whether the man's best pitch is a fastball or whether he relies mostly on breaking stuff. If his specialty is a knuckler or a forkball, he knows that. From talking with teammates who have already batted and from his own observations, he also knows how the pitcher is performing on that particular day, how fast the man is, how much his breaking pitches are breaking, how reliable his control is. The batter is also aware of what strategy the pitcher has used to get him out in previous games. Further, he is aware of his own weakness and what he must do to protect against it.

The batter also knows that the game situation has an influence on what pitches he is going to see and how he must cope with them. What is the score? Is it early in the game or late? Are there any base runners?

Much of this jousting between the hitter and pitcher is centered upon the strike zone, which the rules define as "that space over home plate which is between the batter's armpits and the top of his knees when he assumes his natural stance." As this may imply, the strike zone varies in size depending on the size of the batter, that is, his height and whether or not he crouches. The deeper the crouch, the smaller the strike zone.

Wes Parker faces Tom Seaver.

The strike zone; hitter is Yanks' Bobby Murcer.

Some players claim that the strike zone also varies depending on the league. Frank Robinson, who shuttled back and forth from one league to the other during his long and illustrious career, said that there was more of a tendency on the part of National League umpires to call strikes on low pitches. American League umpires, he said, called the high strike more frequently.

It made for some significant differences. "Since you have to swing at the low strike in the National League, you hit more grounders," said Robinson. "In the American League, swinging at the high strike, you hit more pop-ups.

"The result is that you get more high-average hitters in the National League. Some of those ground balls are going to go through. In the American League, you get more ordinary, low-average hitters who wind up with 15 or 20 homers for the season."

The difference in the size of the strike zone also makes for differences in pitching. In the National League, there is a greater emphasis on breaking-ball and sinking-ball pitches because pitchers have the lower strike zone. In the American League, there's more fastball pitching because of the higher strike zone. Players who have made the switch from

In the National League, relatively low pitches are usually strikes. Here Willie Stargell tries for one.

Ted Williams knew his strike zone perfectly and seldom went for a pitch outside it.

one league to the other call the National League the curveball league.

It is an axiom of baseball that good hitters never swing at anything outside the strike zone. Not only does the hitter put himself at an obvious physical disadvantage any time he swings at a "bad" pitch, he is also working to prevent the ball-strike count from being balanced in his favor.

The success of Ted Williams, often called modern baseball's greatest hitter, was based upon his explicit knowledge of the dimensions of his own strike zone, plus the fact that he would never offer at a pitch outside of it. Indeed, Williams, who compiled a .344 batting average in a 19-year career with the Red Sox, was often criticized for sticking

Managing modern hitters deepened crinkles in Williams' face.

to this principle even when a hit off a bad pitch might have won the ball game.

"No hitter can give anything to a pitcher," Williams insisted. "As soon as the hitter goes for a pitch that's an inch or so outside the strike zone, the pitcher teases him with one that's two inches outside. Pretty soon he's a bad-ball hitter."

In his book, *The Science of Hitting*, Williams consistently stressed this point. "When a batter starts swinging at pitches just two inches out of the strike zone," Williams noted, "he has increased the pitcher's target from approximately 4.2 square feet to about 5.8 square feet—an increase of 37 per cent."

Williams must be listened to. He himself hit .406 in 1941, the highest mark achieved by any hitter in the last half century. He hit 521 home runs, won the American League batting championship six times, played in 18 All-Star games, was twice named the league's Most Valuable Player, and was elected to the Hall of Fame in 1966, the first year he became eligible.

Williams returned to baseball in 1969 as manager of the Washington Senators. (The franchise was later switched to Dallas and became the Texas Rangers.) What did Williams think of the hitters on his team and opposing teams? "The thing that is so appalling to me," he said, "is that so many guys are swinging at bad balls. A good hitter can check a swing. If a guy can't check a swing, then he's got a bat he can't handle." In his first season on the job, Williams guided the Senators to a fourth-place finish and was named Manager of the Year. Then came three seasons of disappointment and frustration, during which time Williams was criticized for his inflexibility in platooning hitters and yanking starting pitchers too early.

But Williams' theories on hitting have seldom, if ever, been questioned. Indeed, just about all of the better hitters support what Williams said. "I agree with Williams completely," said George Sisler, who batted .407 in 1920 and .420 in 1922. "The great hitters just didn't swing at bad pitches. That's why they were great. I know that Babe Ruth wouldn't swing at bad pitches, and neither would Rogers Hornsby."

Joe DiMaggio backed up Williams, too, at least in theory. Said the former Yankee slugger: "A batter never should swing at a bad pitch, but I found myself swinging at bad pitches in an effort to win ball games and thus got into bad habits. But it's wrong and I know it."

Since almost all pitches are just inside or just outside the strike zone, the hitter must, like Ted Williams, have a very specific idea of the dimensions of his own strike zone. The sequence that follows, a typical confrontation between a hitter and pitcher, illustrates.

Imagine it's the ninth inning of a close game. As the hitter, a right-hander, steps up, he pumps the

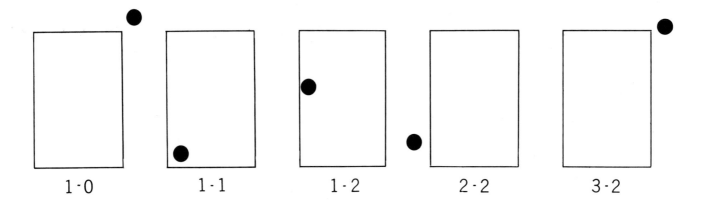

1·0   1·1   1·2   2·2   3·2

bat a few times, cocks it behind his right ear, and eyes the pitcher intently.

Let's suppose that the pitcher is a left-handed curveball specialist. Further, let's suppose the batter's chief weakness is a curve low and away. What he likes are pitches inside and above the waist.

In comes the first pitch, a fastball high and tight. The batter lets it go by. Ball one.

Because the pitch was high and inside, the batter is less inclined to lean in toward the plate. The curveball low and away is now even more of a weakness. So that's what the pitcher throws. It's a slow curve, an abrupt change-of-speed pitch from the fastball just before. The batter, his timing off, swings and misses. Strike one.

The pitcher comes back with a fastball to the outside just below belt level. Even though the batter

anticipated a fastball, the best he can do is foul it off. Strike two.

Now the pitcher can afford to waste a pitch. He throws a curveball low and outside which misses the strike zone by several inches. The batter knows better than to chase it. Ball two.

The pitcher follows with a fastball that's high and in tight. It just misses the plate. It's ball three.

Now the pitcher knows that he must come in with the money pitch, the curveball low and away, putting everything he has on it. The batter is almost certain what the pitch is going to be. He knows the pitcher's strength. He knows his own weakness. He also knows that the pitcher knows it.

Let's say the pitcher puts the ball right where he wants to, and its speed and spin are exactly what he hoped for. What happens? It depends. If the

Jerry Koosman is gloomy after making a pitching mistake. Gene Alley circles the bases.

This is how Willie Mays coped with the brushback.

41

batter simply tries to meet the ball, he can probably push it into left field for a hit. But if he swings from the heels and tries to pull, he is likely to lift a long fly into centerfield, an easy put-out for the center fielder.

As it happens, of course, the pitcher isn't always able to put each pitch precisely where he wants to, nor get exactly the right amount of speed and spin. If he were able to, hitting would be a sad way to make a living. Like schoolteachers and letter carriers, pitchers make mistakes. But pitchers' mistakes end up as home runs.

Besides his assortment of pitches—fastballs, curves, sliders, and change-of-pace throws, or knuckleballs, forkballs, or whatever else he owns—the pitcher has one other weapon at his disposal. Little is said or written about it, but it's as much a part of baseball as the curveball low and away. It's the fastball high and very inside—the brushback.

The brushback isn't meant to hit the batter. It's simply intended to serve as a reminder that a thrown baseball can hurt, even maim. It's meant to intimidate.

The reason for the brushback? The batter has been crowding the plate, leaning into it more than the pitcher likes. By so doing, he is able easily to reach for an outside pitch. The brushback tells the batter to get back where he belongs. The message it relays is almost always heeded.

Generally speaking, hitters bear no ill will toward

Protection comes in a wide range of sizes.

the pitcher who throws high and tight. "I *respect* a pitcher for throwing a knockdown," Hank Aaron once said, "providing that he knows how to control it. Knockdowns are part of the game.

"But what's bad," Aaron added, "is that half of the pitchers don't have control of it. That's the danger."

Occasionally a pitcher will throw directly at a batter, at his body, with the intent of hitting him. It's a means of retaliation. It is almost certain that the opposing pitcher has nicked a batter or two. There comes a time when a team must return like for like. Plunking the ball into the batter's ribs or thigh is often the way the score is evened. "The only way you can protect your teammates," Bob Gibson, the Cards' fastballer, once remarked, "is to

Many players prefer the added protection an earflap helmet gives. This is Ed Brinkman.

retaliate in kind."

Of course, any time a pitcher fires a ball at a batter it represents a breach of the rules. When the umpire believes a pitcher has done so, he is supposed to warn that man that if he does it again he will be ejected. The pitcher can be fined or even suspended. There are cases, of course, of batters being struck by a pitch and being seriously injured. Almost always it's an accident, a case of the pitcher losing control of the throw.

Batting helmets, which became mandatory in 1958, have reduced the chances of a player being seriously hurt, but they have not ruled it out completely. What happens is that the ball strikes the head below the helmet's line of protection. Red Sox star Tony Conigliaro suffered a fractured cheekbone and partial loss of vision in one eye when struck by a pitch in 1967, injuries that hastened his retirement from baseball. Paul Schaal sustained a skull fracture in 1968.

Ron Santo, Don Michner, and Joe Torre are others who have been hit and seriously hurt by pitched balls in recent years. Santo, after he was hit, began to campaign for the use of a protective earflap, in addition to the helmet. Many players now use it.

Only one batter in major league history has been killed by a pitched ball—Roy Chapman of the 1920 Indians. Chapman stood close to the plate and batted from a deep crouch, his head over the

Ron Hunt in an exhibition of his specialty.

plate. Carl Mays was the pitcher who threw the fatal ball. His catcher, Muddy Ruel, insisted that Chapman's head was in the strike zone and that he failed to move as the ball ripped in. "He seemed to freeze," Ruel said afterward. Chapman died the same day, the only major leaguer to die as a result of an injury on the field.

Whenever the subject of being hit by the pitch is under discussion, the name of Ron Hunt comes up. Hunt, an infielder for the Montreal Expos, was hit by the pitch a record 50 times in 1971. It's not that pitchers are particularly unfriendly toward Hunt; it's just that he's in no hurry to move out of the way.

"I crowd the plate, I don't give away any ground, and my first move is into the pitch," Hunt explains. "I hold in there an extra split-second when a lot of other guys are getting out of the way."

Hunt will tell you that there are easier things to do in baseball than stop pitches with your body and he doesn't recommend that Little Leaguers take up the strategy. "It hurts, believe me," he says.

Most of Hunt's "hits" are in the rib area of his left side. "I wish I were a switch-hitter," he has said on several occasions. "New bruises wouldn't be nearly as bad as getting hit on top of old ones."

How does it feel to hold the record for getting hit? "It's not something you brag about," Hunt says. "If you do, they might put you in the loony house."

ADVANCING THE RUNNER

Getting a man on base is one thing. Getting him around to home plate is another. Two standard methods that hitters use to advance the runner are the bunt and the hit-and-run. Each requires different skills.

Most coaches liken the act of bunting to playing catch with the bat. What you have to do, they say, is hold the bat in much the same manner as you hold a glove when awaiting a throw.

Actually, there are two types of bunts, the sacrifice bunt and the type you use when bunting for a base hit. The latter is often called a drag bunt.

When attempting a sacrifice bunt, the batter turns his body so as to face the pitcher, and at the same time slides his upper hand up the bat toward the trademark. He grasps the bat lightly, the thumb on top, the fingers underneath. The other hand remains at the bottom of the bat handle, gripping in such a way that the knuckles face the pitcher.

The idea is to crouch slightly and keep the bat level. If the pitch comes in lower or higher than expected, the batter must either sink lower in the knees or straighten up to meet it. What he shouldn't do is tilt the bat.

When the ball arrives, the batter isn't supposed to punch at it, but simply hold the bat firmly, allow-

A practice bunt by Matty Alou.

45

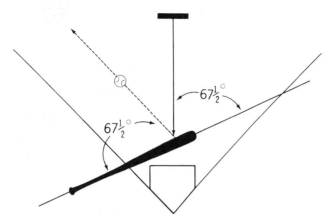

In bunting, the ball leaves the bat at the same angle it strikes it.

Below: **Bill Singer's bunt attempt goes awry, as he pops to Tom Seaver (see next photograph).**

ing the arms and hands to absorb the impact. Even if he's trying to place the ball in a given direction, the batter doesn't have to push it. He doesn't, that is, if he realizes that the ball always leaves the bat at the same angle it meets that bat (although a slight adjustment has to be made for curveballs). For example, suppose the batter wants to bunt down the third-base line. He should hold the bat so that it makes a 67½-degree angle with the ball. The ball will carom from the bat at the same angle, and this puts it precisely down the third-base line (see diagram). Coaches often overlook this basic physical principle when teaching bunting.

One thing that never fails to dismay baseball managers and coaches is the frequent failure of the

46

sacrifice bunt. Bunting seems simple. It's merely a matter of turning to face the pitch and then putting the end of the bat in the path of the ball.

It is simple—during a practice session. But it's not nearly as easy under game conditions, when the pitcher is bearing down in an attempt to prevent the bunt and the first and third basemen dart in to field the ball.

Players practice bunting one or two pitches in the batting cage before they take their regular cuts. But only in spring training do they get to practice bunting under competitive conditions, so it's not unusual that the sacrifice bunt fails so frequently.

Bunting for a base hit requires a different set of techniques. As the pitcher releases, the right-handed hitter has to slide his rear foot back ten or twelve inches from the edge of the plate. The leftie must pivot on the ball of his right foot, then, with his left, take a crossover step toward the pitcher. The advantage to the left-handed batter is obvious; he's a full step closer to first base.

The top hand slides up the bat to the trademark. If the plan is to push the bunt some distance, past the pitcher, say, the top hand should grip firmly. The lower hand guides the bunt's direction.

The hitter should try to make contact with the ball at a point from three to five inches from the bat end. Of course, you try to hit the top half of the ball, so the bunt will go to the ground.

Whenever a team gets a man to third base with less than two out, fans start hoping they'll see a squeeze bunt, one of baseball's most exciting plays. As the pitcher goes into his windup, the base runner rips toward home plate. The batter bunts—and he'd better not miss. If the ball goes by him, it's in the catcher's hands as the runner slides in. If the batter pops it up, and it's caught, it's a sure double play.

It's for these reasons that you don't see the squeeze bunt very often. You can look for it, however, late in a game with the team at bat trailing by a run and there's a man at the plate who has a reputation for striking out frequently.

Bunting has another value, often overlooked. It can be used to keep the infielders "honest." A Yankee coach once noted that infielders were playing slugger Bobby Murcer so deep that they were able to convert into outs ground balls that ordinarily would have been hits. The coach suggested that Bobby begin bunting occasionally to loosen up the infielders. The result was an increase in Murcer's hit production.

Batters of an earlier era not only swung away at the ball and bunted it, they also chopped it. To chop the ball was to swing down on it, employing a quick wrist snap. This caused the ball to strike in front of the plate and rebound in the air. John McGraw, manager of the New York Giants from 1902–1906, spoke highly of the chop in an article he wrote, titled "Some Remarks About Batting for Boys." "If the field be very hard," said McGraw, "frequently the ball will bound so high that it will go over an infielder's head, or it may bound so high that it will be impossible for the fielder to recover it and throw it to first base in time to retire the batter.

"It is a very valuable play at times," McGraw continued, "particularly when the infield happens to be playing close in, desiring to trap a runner who may be trying to score from third. Many a game has been won by a batter who quickly realized the situation, and chopped the ball to the ground rather than making an effort to trust to luck and hit through the infielders."

It must be said that for the batter who choked up the bat, as was the case in McGraw's day, the chop was not a difficult matter. But it is almost impossible to execute when swinging away.

Like the chop, the hit-and-run can be traced to baseball's ragtag days, yet it has remained popular. Actually, the term "hit-and-run" is something of a misnomer. Since the base runner is running—or should be—before the ball is struck, a more appropriate name might be run-and-hit, but that is something different.

The hit-and-run works like this: the third-base coach signals the batter and the runner at first base that the hit-and-run is on. As the pitcher goes into his windup, the runner breaks for second base. The batter then punches the ball to the right side of the infield, behind the runner. The second base-man, assuming that the runner is attempting to steal, darts over to cover the bag, leaving a gaping hole through which the ball bounds. The result is that men end up on first and second base.

You may never have seen the hit-and-run work like this. Don't worry, not many people have. The hit-and-run is seldom successful. In fact, some major league teams don't even use it because it has so many shortcomings. Earl Weaver, manager of the Baltimore Orioles, calls it "the most overrated play in baseball." For one thing, it compels the runner to swing at the pitch in order to protect the runner. If the pitch happens to be bad, an out is the normal result.

Another drawback is that the defensive team is often able to anticipate the hit-and-run, and so they're able to thwart it. The pitcher, for example, will throw outside to a left-handed batter. If he tries to hit such a pitch to the right side, he's very likely to pop it up. Since the runner has broken for second base, there's a possibility of a double play.

If the catcher believes a hit-and-run has been signaled, he can call for a pitchout, the idea being to nail the runner at second. Then the hitter's task of protecting the runner becomes almost impossible. He may have to lunge at the ball, attempting at the very least to foul it off.

Some batters have exceptional bat control and, therefore, are skilled in executing the hit-and-run. Jerry Grote of the Mets, for instance, could watch the infielders, and if the second baseman moved to cover second, Grote would rap the ball toward the right side, hopefully through the area vacated by the man. If the shortstop moved to cover, Grote would hit to the left side.

Sometimes you may see what looks to be a hit-and-run, but it's not. It's a more subtle piece of strategy called the run-and-hit. The runner is given a signal that he can run on the pitch if he feels he can get a good jump; he doesn't *have* to run.

The batter is on his own, too. He may or may not swing to protect the runner. If he sees that the runner has gotten a good jump and it looks like he is going to make second base safely, the batter will let the pitch go by (as long as the count is less than two strikes). But if the batter doesn't think the runner is going to make it, he'll swing.

The matter of advancing base runners and scoring runs is uppermost in the manager's mind when it comes to making out the day's batting order. He seeks to arrange his hitters in such a way that the team will derive maximum benefit from their individual talents.

The leadoff man has to be a sticky hitter, skilled at getting on base and a good man on the base paths. He doesn't have to be a power hitter.

The second man in the batting order should be adept at advancing the runner. He has to be able to bunt; he has to know how to execute the hit-and-run, hitting to right field or, when necessity de-

Bobby Bonds rates as one of baseball's best leadoff men.

mands, letting the pitch go by. He has to be a good runner.

If the first two men perform in the way they are

expected to, the No. 3 man comes to bat with a runner, perhaps two, on base. It's then his job to drive them home. That's why the No. 3 man is the best hitter on the team, the player with the highest average and also something of a power hitter.

The No. 4 man in the batting order, the so-called clean-up hitter, is the team's best slugger. He usually has more home runs and runs batted in than any of the other players.

The No. 5 and No. 6 men are also able to "clean" the bases with one swing, although they seldom have the consistency of the No. 4 man. These men sometimes lack in running speed, too.

The No. 7 and No. 8 men in the lineup are weaker hitters. Frequently they are in the lineup because of their fielding skills, not what they can accomplish at the plate. It is not easy to be this far down in the lineup, because pitchers look at the No. 7 and No. 8 hitters as sure outs and often bear down hard on them.

Pitchers always bat last (except when the designated hitter rule is in effect, in which case they don't bat at all). It's a tradition that managers are especially reluctant to violate, even when they have a good-hitting pitcher on hand. Perhaps they recall what happened to Lou Boudreau, manager of the Boston Red Sox in 1954. One of Boudreau's pitchers that season was Mel Parnell, a better-than-average hitter. Boudreau had Parnell hit seventh in the lineup, ahead of weaker batsmen. The Red

The punch—the number 4 and 5 hitters—in the A's lineup.

Sox had one of their worst seasons in years and before it ended Boudreau was fired.

Besides these, there are many other considerations. Of prime importance is the pitcher the team is to face. Is he a right-hander or a left-hander? Are there particular hitters that he is effective against? Which hitters do well against him? Most teams keep detailed records as to how each of their batters has performed against each pitcher in the league, and this statistical data often carries much weight in deciding who will play and who will sit on the bench.

Suppose the Orioles are facing the Yankees and Mel Stottlemyre is to pitch for New York. On the morning of the game, Baltimore manager Earl Weaver is given a comprehensive statistical breakdown that discloses how each of his players has batted against Stottlemyre, both for the season and over their careers. Each man's at-bats and batting average are given, as are the number of times he's singled, doubled, tripled, hit a home run, walked, or struck out. The chart takes much of the guesswork out of making up the lineup. It can happen that Weaver will have a .400 hitter batting No. 7 or No. 8, that is, the man will have earned a .400 average in hitting *against Stottlemyre*.

Injuries are a factor in making out the lineup card. Fatigue is, too. During the final weeks of the season, players begin to need a day off once in a while. The best time to rest a man is when a day

52

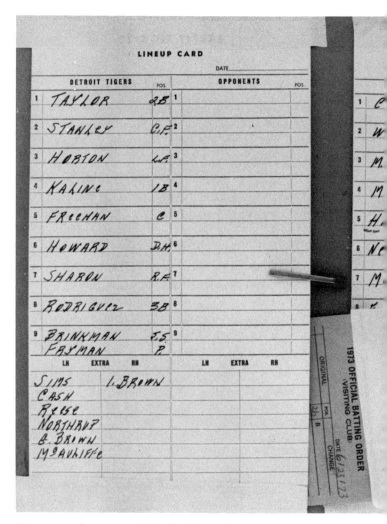

Lineup card as posted in the Tiger dugout.

game follows a night game. But again it depends on who's pitching. No man will be given a day off if the starting pitcher happens to be one he hits particularly well—nor would he want to sit out the contest.

The manager also has to be sure that the lineup gives him adequate defensive strength. A consistent hitter who is slow in the outfield and has a weak arm becomes questionable as a starter.

A man's speed is always a consideration. For example, Brooks Robinson of the Orioles was slow on the base paths, so manager Earl Weaver would try to put a fast man in the batting order just in front of Robinson. This helped to rule out a double play when Robinson came to the plate.

It is one of the fundamentals of baseball that a right-handed batter will have better results against a left-handed pitcher than he will against a right-handed one, and that a left-handed batter will do his best against right-handed pitching. In making up the batting order, some managers follow this axiom unfailingly, while others realize that each hitter-pitcher confrontation is different, and although the rule is generally true it is subject to frequent exceptions.

Suppose you are a right-handed hitter and a left-hander happens to be pitching. Since he delivers the ball from the first-base side of the mound, you're able to get the ball into your field of vision without any difficulty. This makes it easier for you to judge the ball's speed and trajectory, easier than when a right-hander is on the mound and you have to turn your head in order to see the pitch being released.

Another reason that the right-handed batter does better against a leftie pitcher has to do with the ball's spin. The natural spin a pitcher imparts to a thrown ball makes it curve away from the side from which it is thrown. A curve thrown by a left-handed pitcher breaks toward a right-handed hitter, which is easier to cope with than a curve that breaks away.

If any player has ever spoken well about his manager's decision to use him only against the right-handed or left-handed pitching—that is, to platoon him—the man's name has been lost to history. No one wants to be in the lineup one day and out of it the next. "You gotta play every day to do your best," is the often-heard argument.

"But you can't play against left-handed pitching," the manager will say, "because you can't hit it."

"How am I going to learn to hit left-handers," the player answers, "if you never use me against them?"

It's an argument that has little weight, as can be judged by the large number of players who are platooned.

The next time you're at a baseball game and a

During 1973, left-hander Ron Blomberg hit only against right-handed pitchers. Here he faces Marty Pattin.

batter steps up to the plate with men on base in a crucial situation, don't watch the batter; watch the third-base coach. He will seem to be afflicted, furiously fidgeting and wigwagging as he shouts words of encouragement to the hitter. He pulls at the peak of his cap, strokes his cheek, brushes the letters on his uniform, tightens his belt, folds his arms and then unfolds them, and he does all of these things in rapid-fire succession before the first pitch is thrown.

What the coach is doing, of course, is giving signals, and thereby instructing the batter what he is to do. He may be ordering him to bunt or to play hit-and-run, or he may be instructing him to "take" the pitch or hit away. (The "take" sign means "Do not swing at the next pitch," while the hit sign says, "Go ahead and swing *if* the pitch is a good one.")

To confuse the opposition, teams camouflage the valid signal with several that have no meaning. Suppose Bud Harrelson is at bat for the Mets. There's a runner on first base with one out. The score is tied. Before Harrelson steps in, he looks toward Eddie Yost in the third-base coach's box. In the space of two or three seconds, Yost claps his hands, adjusts his cap, scuffs the dirt with his spikes, and puts his hand to his chin. Harrelson now knows what to do—bunt. When Yost scuffed the dirt, he was flashing the bunt sign. All of the other signals were meaningless, intended only to disguise the real sign.

Many teams use what's called an indicator sign to inform the batter that the real sign is coming. Before the game, the players will be told that all signs are without meaning until the coach tugs at the peak of his cap. That's the indicator. It means that the valid signal is the next one.

Sometimes the feet are used to flash the indicator. The batter will be instructed, for example, not to pay attention to any sign unless one of the coach's feet is touching a coaching-box chalk line.

Leo Durocher once used a set of signals that were based, not on how the coach signaled, but how often. The batter would count the number of signs flashed. If only one sign was given, a bunt was being ordered. Two signs meant to take the pitch, three meant hit-and-run, and so on.

If the coach feels that the batter is uncertain about what he should be doing, he will call a time-out and hold a private conference with the man, whispering the instructions into his ear. When you see this happen, it may not be what it seems to be, however. It is sometimes a tactical maneuver, meant to rattle a pitcher who is going strong.

The instructions given the batter almost never originate with the third-base coach himself. He is only relaying the manager's commands. It's up to the coach to look into the dugout and "read" what the manager wants before each pitch. It used to be that managers stationed themselves at third base

Red Sox coach Eddie Popowski goes through his repertoire of signals.

Yankees' Horace Clarke gets his instructions from coach Dick Howser.

and signalled the batter directly. But those of the present day prefer to remain in the dugout, where it's warmer in the spring and fall, cooler in the summer, and always quieter and calmer.

Players in the dugout sometimes try to steal the opposition's signals, but it's not easy. It takes two men, one to watch the third-base coach, the other to watch the runner. Their commentary sounds like this:

"He's brushing the letters on his shirt," says the man who's watching the coach.

"He's looking at the pitcher," says the man who's covering the runner.

"He's clapping his hands."

"He's taking a lead; he's three steps off the base."

"He's hitching his belt."

"He's looking back at first.

And so it goes, with the two trying to establish some relationship between the coach's gestures and the action taken by the runner. If the two men are able to break the code, the results can be very profitable. Charley Dressen, a manager and coach for three decades, and one of the best counterspies in the business, claimed one season to have stolen signs and called pitches that accounted for nine of his team's victories.

57

Players constantly practice the skills necessary to advance runners, and managers hold team meetings frequently to explain strategy. But sometimes all the effort has to be questioned. Take what happened in a World Series recently. The year was 1971, Pittsburgh vs. Baltimore. In the seventh inning of game three, up to the plate for the Pirates stepped Bob Robertson, hitless in two previous contests, both won by the Orioles. Two runners were on base. The bunt sign was flashed.

Robertson never saw it. Instead of bunting, he lashed into one of Mike Cuellar's screwballs, powdering a drive that cleared the fence in right center field at Three Rivers Stadium. The blow put the game out of the Orioles' reach, and the revitalized Pirates went on to win the series in seven games.

When Robertson crossed home plate, Willie Stargell, who had been on base, was waiting to shake his hand. "That's the way to bunt," said Stargell.

IMPROVING

Harry Walker, batting instructor for the St. Louis Cardinals, has made a lifetime study of the art of hitting. He has read whatever has been written on the subject, interviewed the best hitters and listened to their theories, and filmed many of them with the special sequence camera he owns. He was no slouch as a hitter himself, having led the National League in 1947 with a .363 average.

"Hitting," says Walker, "is a learned art." It's his belief that any hitter can improve his average through proper instruction and practice. Walker also believes that some hitters are particularly gifted, men like Ted Williams and Stan Musial. "But even they," Walker declares, "can improve by work, work, work."

Declining batting averages and the resulting low scoring have caused clubs to pay more attention to hitting instruction. Most teams now have sophisticated training aids available for use by their players on a year-round basis, and hitting coaches like Harry Walker are enjoying a more lofty status than ever before.

Harry Walker's older brother, Dixie, a star with the Brooklyn Dodgers in the 1940s, is batting coach for the Los Angeles Dodgers. The Walkers follow a standard procedure in instruction. The idea is to first observe a batter carefully, then make

Dodgers' Dixie Walker (right), pictured here with Willie Davis, is one of baseball's most highly regarded hitting instructors.

59

Harry Walker, here being interviewed by sportscaster Ron Jacober—"Hitting is a learned art."

recommendations for changes in the man's stance or swing.

But it's not easy. Most hitters are reluctant to try anything new. They feel that whatever success they happen to have achieved is the direct result of hitting the ball in a certain way, and they would rather cling to that style than attempt a technique that's different and which might possibly result in failure.

"If you could give a weak hitter a tip that would lift his average 20 or 30 points in the span of a couple of weeks, there would be no difficulties," Harry Walker says, "but instant success is almost impossible. The process of improving is gradual. It takes months.

"Often when a hitter tries something new, his average dips for a while. He has to be able to suffer through this period. But not all hitters can. They get hot and they say, 'You got me all screwed up,' and they go back to their usual style.

"There are a lot of .240 hitters around who should be hitting .260 or .270, a lot of .280 hitters who could be up above .300. But they have to make changes and they don't have the courage or confidence to do so."

Walker points to Matty Alou as his prize pupil. Alou hit .231 in 1965. After listening to Walker's lectures and following his instruction advice, Alou, the very next year, became the National League batting champion, hitting .342.

Many hitters seek to improve their proficiency on

their own during the pregame ritual known as batting practice, but most coaches claim this exercise is, at best, of dubious value. For batting practice to be at all meaningful to a hitter, he has to be fed an assortment of fastballs, curves, and sliders, just as he is in a game. But many players want only half-speed pitches down the middle, so they can try to belt the ball out of the park. This is good exercise for the hands, arms, and shoulders but it really doesn't do much toward improving one's hitting skills.

"There are a lot of guys who hit 400 or more home runs in batting practice during the year, but in game competition they hit only four or five," says Chuck Tanner, manager of the White Sox. "And in trying to knock every ball into the next county, they get into had habits, lunging and jerking their heads. Results are what count, not what you do in practice."

Dick Allen of the White Sox, the leading hitter in the American League in recent years, is one of the growing number of players who believes that the value of pregame batting practice is overrated. Once he's in shape for the season, Allen will go weeks without entering the batting cage. He feels, in view of the 162-game schedule, the enormous number of night games, and the other rigors the season imposes, that rest is more beneficial than practice swings. "A few throws in front of the dug-out and I'm ready to go," Allen says. "I'll get my

swings in the on-deck circle—and then in the batter's box." Of course, in the case of a hitter in a slump or one who needs to correct a flaw that's been detected in his swing, the batting cage has value.

Virtually all teams today offer players the benefits to be derived from video-tape instruction. Video-tape units record television images on wide magnetic tape. Tapes are first made when the batter is hitting the ball well. Should the man fall into a slump, a new tape is made. This is compared with the first tape, and then the manager, or a coach,

Most coaches agree that batting practice has only limited value.

Kansas City Royals check a taped playback with hitting coach Charlie Lau (second from left). Pictured (left to right) are Joe Keough, Lau, Lou Piniella, and Jerry May.

and the batter try to discover what the man is doing that's different.

Another device teams use to help hitters is the pitching machine. You yourself may have seen machines of this type at an amusement park batting range. A supply of balls is fed automatically one-by-one into the machine's long steel arm. The arm snaps quickly forward, catapulting the ball toward the plate. At baseball training camps in the spring,

pitching machines are available for hitting practice from sunup to sundown.

The Philadelphia Phillies recently installed a pitching machine and a batting cage in an underground driveway beneath Veterans Stadium. It can be used by any player who wants extra practice. Players who live near the stadium are invited to use the cage during the winter months, and many do.

Pitching machines have become quite sophisticated. They can be adjusted to throw high or low strikes, or inside or outside pitches. They can throw a wide variety of pitches—fastballs (at a speed of

Pitching machines are a standard training aid.

up to 98 miles per hour), curves, and even change-of-pace pitches. They can be operated by a coach or made to pitch automatically at the rate of about one ball every 9 or 10 seconds.

While the pitching machine has value as a training aid, it is not without its limitations. What it does is duplicate the path a ball takes on its way to the hitter. What it doesn't do is duplicate the pitcher's windup. Part of every pitcher's success results from the deceptiveness of his arm and leg motion, and the hitter using the batting machine gets no schooling in how to cope with these.

A hitter who is having no problems is likely to be indifferent to the various instruction aids available to him, but should he fall into a slump it's a different story. Then he wants the coach's assistance, his swing analyzed by means of video tape, and extra work in the batting cage. The problem with slumps is that they are usually caused by something quite minor, so insignificant the player himself can't detect it.

During 1972, Ken Henderson, then with the San Francisco Giants, started off the season poorly at the plate, then went downhill. On August 1 his batting average was a sad .195. Then coach John McNamara noticed that Henderson wasn't holding the bat in his normal manner. He had altered the position of his hands so that he was holding the bat almost vertical as he awaited the pitch. McNamara got Henderson to adjust his grip, to flatten the bat.

The tip enabled Henderson to add more than 60 points to his batting average before the season ended.

One of the most notable slumps of recent years befell not individuals but almost an entire team, the Baltimore Orioles. In 1971 the Orioles breezed to their third consecutive division title, beating out the second-place Detroit Tigers by twelve games.

The team tumbled to third place in 1972, chiefly because they were never able to generate any offense. Hitters who were used to manhandling American League pitching turned anemic. Here is a year-to-year comparison of averages:

	1971	1972
Andy Etchebarren	.270	.202
Mark Belanger	.266	.186
John (Boog) Powell	.256	.252
Brooks Robinson	.272	.250
Paul Blair	.262	.233
Don Buford	.290	.206
Merv Rettenmund	.318	.233

The team's batting average for the season was a woeful .229, down from .261 from the year before. No Oriole regular managed to hit .300, drive in 100 runs, or hit 25 home runs.

It was an agonizing year for Baltimore manager Earl Weaver and batting coach Jim Frey. Weaver talked with hitters individually and in groups, and ordered countless sessions of extra batting practice. Nothing seemed to work.

"There seems no rhyme or reason or cause for it," moaned Weaver toward the end of the year. "It just happens. It doesn't matter who is out there pitching for the other team. It doesn't matter if he throws a fastball, curve, knuckler, or spitter. We miss them all."

As this implies, there is still much to be learned about the science of hitting a thrown baseball. Further evidence is the great army of major leaguers who never manage to hit more than .230 for a season, and not the magic of video tape, countless hours in the batting cage, nor the personal assistance of Harry Walker will ever reform them.

Orioles' hitting slump bewildered manager Earl Weaver. Here he studies Boog Powell.

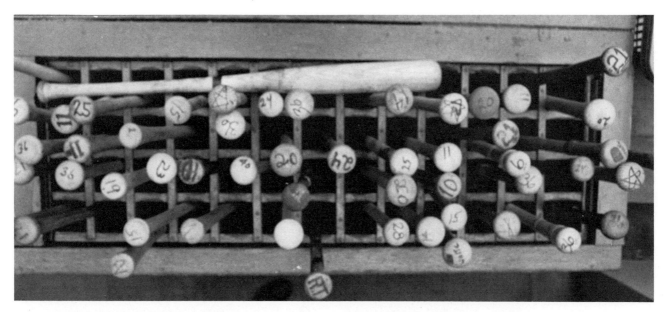

Bats used by the New York Yankees. Numbers correspond to player uniform numbers.

ALL ABOUT BATS

John Hillerich of Hillerich & Bradsby, the company that makes the Louisville Slugger, once put six bats on a bed, one of them a half an ounce heavier than the others. He then asked Ted Williams to close his eyes and pick out the heavier bat. Williams did—twice in a row.

Not every major league hitter is as sensitive as Ted Williams used to be as to the bat's size, shape,

length, and weight. But to each man these are topics of crucial importance.

A player has a good deal of latitude in choosing a bat. All the rules say is that the bat "shall be a smooth, rounded stick, not more than 2¾ inches in diameter at the thickest part and not more than 42 inches in length."

About 95 per cent of all bats are made of ash, a hard, close-grained, somewhat elastic wood. Polo mallets and some hockey sticks are also made of ash. What makes ash superior to other woods is its resiliency, its whippiness. When the batter's swing is timed right, the bat snaps into the ball, and this boosts significantly the power of the swing.

Trees from which bats are made are found in relatively limited areas of the Northeast, in the southern part of New York State, near the Pennsylvania border, and in northern Pennsylvania. Trees that grow on the northern and easterly slopes of mountains usually produce the best bats. A tall, straight tree, 40 to 50 years of age, will make about 60 bats.

Hillerich & Bradsby of Louisville, Kentucky, is the biggest bat company in the world, producing almost five million bats a year. The company's Louisville Sluggers are used by Little Leaguers and major leaguers and by all of the countless categories of players in between.

The firm got started in the bat business by accident. The J. F. Hillerich Company, as it was originally known, was founded in 1856, and specialized in wood-turning, in the production of a variety of wooden shapes, such as tenpins and wooden bowling balls, bed posts, porch columns, and newel posts for staircases.

In 1880, the owner's son, John (Bud) Hillerich, not long out of grade school, joined the company as an apprentice wood-turner. Bud was a baseball fan, and one summer afternoon in 1884 he was watching his favorite team, the Louisville Eclipses

of the American Association, when Pete Browning, the team's star slugger, broke his favorite bat. Young Hillerich sought out Browning after the game and offered to make him a replacement.

The two went to Hillerich's shop, and there Browning picked out a length of ash and Bud went to work on it. Several times the wood was removed from the lathe to allow Browning a few test swings. "A little off here and a little off there," Browning would suggest. Finally, he judged the weapon to be "just right."

The next day Pete Browning got three hits in three trips to the plate, and the day after that his teammates began showing up at the Hillerich shop. Before the season ended, members of other teams in the league had become customers. Bats represented a major portion of Hillerich's business by the turn of the century.

The use of signatures on bats dates to 1905, the year Honus Wagner signed an endorsement contract. Ty Cobb's autographed bat appeared in 1908, and one bearing the name of Frank (Home Run) Baker in 1911.

Then, as now, the manufacturer is careful to stamp the endorser's autograph on the flat of the grain. The "real punch" of a bat, says Hillerich & Bradsby, is derived by hitting off the side of the grain. Putting the signature—and the label—on the flat of the grain enables a player to tell at a glance whether he is holding the bat correctly. All he has

Weaponry used by the Baltimore Orioles includes a length of steel reinforcing rod. But it's only for swinging when warming up.

to do is "keep the trademark up." Hitting on the side of the grain also reduces the chance of chipping or splitting the wood.

No matter what the ultimate use of the bat, sandlot play or the major leagues, each one follows somewhat the same manufacturing process. The selected trees are felled, stripped of their branches, and the trunks are hauled to a timber mill. There they are sawed into 40-inch lengths, each of which is known as a "bolt." The bolts are then split lengthwise into sections called, appropriately, "splits." Next, each split is put onto a lathe and its roughness cut away. Known by the general term "billets," the rounded shapes are shipped by rail to the manufacturing plant.

There the billets are examined and graded by inspectors, then stacked in tall piles. The stacking is done in such a way that air can circulate through each pile. Months of drying out, of seasoning, fol-

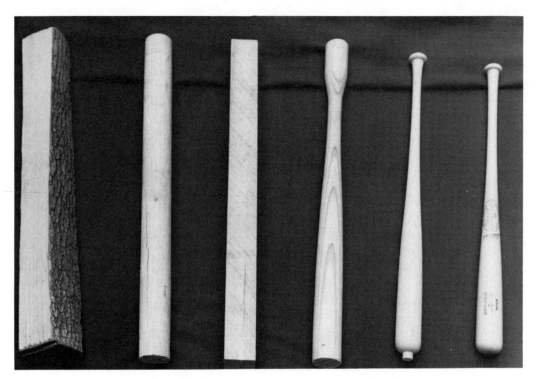

Production stages from a "split" to finished bat.

low. Hillerich & Bradsby always have at least four million billets undergoing seasoning in the company's ten-acre timber yard. The billets are inspected periodically and any that develop flaws are discarded.

How long a period each billet remains in the timber yard depends on the characteristics of the wood at the time of cutting and the type of weather to which it is exposed. A cold winter hastens the seasoning process. The time period can very from 10 to 18 months.

Hillerich & Bradsby maintains a card file containing the bat specifications for thousands of major league and minor league players. In addition, original models of the bats are kept locked in a fireproof vault.

Suppose the company receives an order from the Chicago White Sox for twelve bats for Dick Allen. An experienced judge of bat wood removes Allen's model from the vault and takes it to the seasoned timber supply where he selects billets that match it in quality and weight. In the turning room, a skilled craftsman duplicates the original model on a hand lathe. After being turned, the bat is trimmed, sanded, lacquered, polished, and branded with the company trademark and Allen's signature. The new bats measure and weigh exactly the same as the original. Thus, Dick Allen won't have to spend time getting used to their feel and swing.

Players who are extremely particular about their bats can visit the plant and personally select billets. Ted Williams used to do this, combing the timber yard for the special narrow-grained wood that he preferred. Williams once rejected several bats because the handles were 1/100 of an inch smaller than those he specified.

Only a tiny percentage of bats receive the meticulous handcrafted treatment described above. Bats destined for amateur leagues or those to be sold in sporting goods stores are turned out using mass-production techniques.

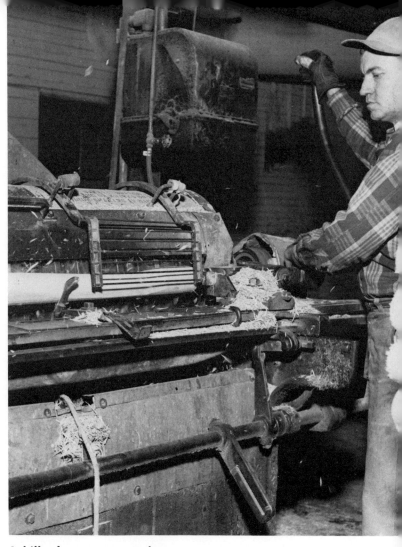

A billet becomes a roughout.

69

Billets are put one by one onto semiautomatic lathes and "roughed out," that is, turned into a length of wood of approximately bat size and bat weight (see photograph). The roughouts are inspected and weighed to determine the model bat for which each is best suited.

The roughout is mounted on a lathe, and in a matter of seconds is cut and shaped into an authentic copy of a major leaguer's model. The bat is then machine-sanded, trimmed, lacquered, and "autographed."

Bats being manufactured nowadays bear only a vague resemblance to those of the past century. During the 1880s and 1890s, bats were, by today's standards, relatively shapeless. With their thick handles and big barrels, they had a clublike appearance. By the turn of the century, handles had become smaller but barrels were bigger. These bats were short, averaging about 34 inches.

Bigger bats were the order of the day in Babe Ruth's time. They weighed 42 to 44 ounces, and the Babe himself used a 48-ouncer. As Ruth grew older, however, he used progressively lighter bats, and in 1927, the year he hit his record 60 home runs, he was down to 40 ounces.

By comparison, the bats used by today's major leaguers are real lightweights, with most of them weighing 35 ounces or less. They are almost always less than 36 inches in length. Here are some examples: Pete Rose, Joe Torre, and Willie Stargell, 35

Roughouts await sorting and grading.

Bats of the early 1900s had large handles, small price tags.

inches and 35 ounces; Johnny Bench, 35 inches, 32½ ounces; and Hank Aaron, 35 inches, 33 ounces.

Of course, not all players follow the trend. Dick Allen uses a 40-ounce bat, one of the heaviest presently being manufactured by Hillerich & Bradsby. It's 35 inches in length. Allen does not recommend a bat of this type to young hitters, however.

Many players change bats during the season, some shifting to a model that's an ounce or so lighter in weight as the end of the playing schedule draws near. Pete Rose, for example, drops to a 33-ounce bat. Billy Williams uses a bat that's 34½ inches in length, but orders two different weights, a 33-ounce model for spring training and a 32-ouncer that he uses once the season starts. Bench, Torre, and Stargell keep to the same weight and length of bat throughout the season.

Some hitters vary bat weight depending on the type of pitching they're facing. Garry Maddox uses a 34½-ounce bat against left-handed pitching, a 33½-ounce bat against right-handers.

It's not just the bat's length and weight that concerns the major league player. He also is careful about the circumference of the bat handle and barrel, the amount of taper between the two and the size of the knob at the handle end. The handle size

is particularly important. With a thick-handled bat, the hitter has a slower swing because he can't roll his wrists as readily as he follows through. Thick-handled bats are for slapping the ball, for making contact. To whip the bat around, as the modern player likes to do, a thin handle is what's needed.

Johnny Bench, for example, wants a bat with a small barrel that tapers gradually to a small handle. He also specifies a knob of medium size. Richie Scheinblum has been successful using a bat without any knob at all. It ends in a cone handle. He says a knob gives him blisters.

Hank Aaron had a bat with a medium-size barrel and medium-size handle and a normal taper. The knob was a bit larger than normal size. Mickey Mantle's bat had a large barrel that tapered normally to a handle of medium size. He liked a large knob.

No matter what style of bat you yourself use, you don't have to hit many pitches before you realize that there is a certain spot on the bat that produces a sharper hit than any other spot. When the ball strikes this spot, there's a clear, sharp, high-pitched sound. And it feels like a solid hit; there's no sting.

Most players think that this spot is the bat's center of gravity, but it's not. By name, the spot is the

Dick Allen uses a 40-ounce bat, heaviest of all major leaguers.

bat's "center of percussion." It is the spot on the bat where the momentum of the batter's swing is transferred to the ball with the greatest possible efficiency.

The center of percussion is usually to be found at a point two to ten inches from the thick end of the bat. When the ball is struck on one side or the other of the center of percussion, the bat tries to swing around that point. The twisting force that results causes the bat to oscillate, a phenomenon the batter experiences by sharp, smarting pain— sting. The farther the ball is struck from the center of percussion, the greater the sting.

Any time a bat stings your hands, it's a sign that energy is being wasted. The ball is not going to travel the greatest possible distance.

You can get longer, sharper hits, and avoid bat sting, by always hitting the ball at the bat's center of percussion. To find this spot, grip the bat as you do when hitting, and then have a friend tap the bat with a rubber-covered hammer (or any other instrument that won't dent the bat) at points one inch apart over the length of the bat. Have him begin the series of taps at the bat's thick end. As he taps, you will find a particular spot where the tapping does not cause any vibration or sting. A blow there has a solid sound, a sharp *thwack*. This

In spring training Billy Williams uses a heavier bat than during the regular season.

Richie Scheinblum uses a unique cone-handled bat (inset).

is the bat's center of percussion. Mark it with a crayon.

Of course, it's not just the bat and the power with which it's swung that determines how far a batted ball will travel. A third important factor is the speed, the velocity, with which the pitched ball travels. A fastball comes off the bat much faster than a "junk" pitch (the momentum of the swings being equal).

When a bat hits a baseball, the ball is pressed out of perfect roundness for a fraction of a second by the force of the bat. As the ball goes back to its original shape, it acts in springlike fashion, jumping off the bat. The greater the ball's speed as it comes toward the bat, the more it will be squeezed out of shape and, thus, the greater its recoil off the bat.

This principle is easy to prove. Throw a fastball against the side of a building or a brick wall. Then throw a slower pitch. Note the greater rebound of the fastball.

In the past decade or so, bat manufacturers have been seeking other materials that have the same characteristics as close-grained white ash. To a degree, they have been successful. Of the estimated 10 million bats sold in 1971, somewhat more than

It's obvious that Bobby Murcer's bat gets plenty of attention.

half a million were manufactured of something other than wood.

Next to wood, aluminum is the most popular material. The weights and lengths of aluminum bats are the same as those of wood. The advantage of aluminum is one of durability; an aluminum bat will never crack or splinter. Early models of aluminum bats gave off a tinny ping when the ball was struck, but manufacturers corrected this by filling the bat core with plastic foam. Present-day aluminum bats duplicate the solid thwack of the wooden bat.

Aluminum bats come in a rainbow of different colors but all have a metallic look to them. They have been approved for Little League use and by the NCAA for college competition.

Nylon bats, introduced in amateur play in the 1970s, look like wood bats and sound like wood, and only by close inspection can you tell them apart. Yet they are as unbreakable as bats of aluminum. Magnesium bats, advertised as being made of "a space-age metal," have many of the characteristics of aluminum bats. Both nylon and magnesium bats have been approved for Little League play.

As of 1974, bats used in major league competition were uniformly of wood. But most observers feel that change is coming—just as it has to in other sports. In pole vaulting, the pole used to be bamboo; now it's fiberglass. Skis made of wood may be going the way of the buggy whip.

Aluminum bats are popular with Little Leaguers.

Major league rules now say that the bat must be made of wood, and wood exclusively. However, when today's Little Leaguers and college players begin arriving in the major leagues, it is almost certain that they will campaign for changes in the rules that will permit the bat to be something more than merely a "rounded *stick*."

THE GAME SAVERS

To pinch-hit, says the dictionary, means "to bat in the place of a player scheduled to bat, especially when a hit is badly needed." The words "badly needed" understate the situation; *desperately* needed is closer to the truth.

This is the chief reason that most pinch-hitters are players with more than an average amount of experience. You have to be relaxed and confident. You have to know the pitcher, his technique, his strategy, and you have to know the strike zone.

Gates Brown of the Detroit Tigers ranked as one of the most dependable pinch-hitters of recent years. Brown said that patience is the most important quality a pinch-hitter can have. "The idea is to make the pitcher come to you," he declared, "which is what he's got to do if you wait."

When Brown went to the plate, he was thinking about the game situation, and how it affected what he was supposed to do. "If it's a tie game, one out and a man on third base, I don't have to go for a base hit. All I have to do is get the ball to the outfield so the man on third can score after the catch.

"If the bases are empty, then I'll go for the long ball and hope home run. In most other cases, I'm content to meet the ball where it's pitched."

Not every pitcher has the emotional makeup to come out of the bullpen and perform in the clutch; so, too, not every hitter can be expected to go up to

"Make the pitcher come to you," says Gates Brown.

Brown has a tip for the Yankees' batboy.

the plate under pressure and deliver a hit. It requires a special temperament, the ability to remain calm despite the tenseness of the situation.

Did anything ever upset Gates Brown? The answer is yes. "One thing that bothers me," Brown once said, "is when I come up with a runner on second, one out, and first base open—and the opposing manager doesn't order me walked!

"You've *got* to walk a guy in a situation like that, so you can go for the double play. And when a rival manager doesn't do it, it beats me mentally."

Slumps hit pinch-hitters, just as they do men who play every day. How did Brown cope with a sudden decline in his ability to hit? "Whenever I lose my timing at the plate," he said, "I always ask the manager for a start in the outfield. I know when my swing is messed up and I know how to correct it. Once I get into a game and see living pitching three or four times, I'm all right again. It works every time."

The Babe Ruth—or Hank Aaron—of pinch-hitters was Forrest (Smokey) Burgess, originally a catcher, who toiled for the Cubs, Phillies, Reds, Pirates, and White Sox in a career that stretched 18 seasons. During 1966, Burgess reached first base 36 times in his role as a pinch-hitter, an all-time record. And, as *The Little Red Book of Baseball* also notes, Burgess holds the record for most pinch-hits—lifetime, 144. It's a record that seems as "safe" as Joe DiMaggio's 56-game hitting streak.

Smokey Burgess, premier pinch-hitter.

Smokey Burgess didn't look like a baseball player is supposed to look. He was 5-foot-8, 195 pounds, and in the latter stages of his career moved with a distinct waddle. A pinch-runner for pinch-hitter Burgess was standard procedure.

While his physique was considerably less than the ideal, Burgess had the perfect temperament for a pinch-hitter. It didn't matter to him whether the pitcher was left-handed or right-handed. (He himself happened to be a leftie batter.) It didn't make any difference whether he went up to the plate early in the game or late, or whether or not there were men on the bases. He could punch hits over the infield or lash the ball just inside the foul line. "A hit's a hit," he once said. "That's all there is to the game of baseball."

Burgess liked to swing at the first pitch. This was his reasoning: "The pitcher's gonna come in right away with your best pitch because he wants to get you swinging. You aren't going to see that good pitch again because the pitcher is going to give you *his* best pitch from then on, not yours."

Burgess, like most of the best pinch-hitters, regarded taking a called third strike as an unpardonable sin, and probably would have preferred a cutback in meal money to being the victim of one. "It's a hanging offense," he said.

While baseball's record book pays frequent tribute to the exploits of Smokey Burgess, historical accounts of the role of the pinch hitter never fail to feature the name of James Lamar (Dusty) Rhodes, a farm boy from Mathews, Alabama, who played for the New York Giants during a brief span in the mid-1950s. In the 1954 World Series, Rhodes single-handedly destroyed the Cleveland Indians for Leo Durocher's crew, and he did it as pinch hitter.

In the bottom half of the tenth inning of the opening game, played at New York's Polo Grounds, the score was deadlocked, 2–2, when Rhodes was sent up to hit for Monte Irvin. Willie Mays was on second base, Hank Thompson on first. Bob Lemon went into his windup and tossed a slow curve that hung a bit, and Rhodes lofted the pitch into the air, but deep enough so that it just managed to reach the right-field stands. It marked only the second time in baseball history that a batter had pinch-hit a homer in a World Series game.

The very next afternoon, Rhodes pinch-hit in the fifth inning, and this time he singled, driving in a run that tied the score. Durocher sent him to the outfield for the rest of the game, and Rhodes responded by hitting another home run in the eighth inning. The final score: New York, 3; Cleveland, 1.

The script for the third game, played in Cleveland, was very similar. Rhodes was sent in to pinch-hit and he poked a single into right field on the first pitch, driving in two runs. Again the Giants won.

Three games. Three pinch-hits by Rhodes. Three Giant victories. Understandably, Cleveland's pitching came apart in the fourth game, and the New Yorkers won with ease.

World Series hero Dusty Rhodes.

The New York press went into hysterics over the Giants' instant hero. But the biggest headlines Rhodes earned came during the third game when he happened to strike out. Newspapers ran photos of him swinging and missing. Rhodes striking out—that was *real* news!

In 1973, in an effort to pep up the game, the American League voted into being a rule that gave new lustre to the art of pinch-hitting—the designated hitter rule. It represented the first major revision in playing rules since 1920, the year that the spitball was made illegal.

In effect, the rule permits a manager to add a tenth man to his starting lineup. The designated hitter, or "dh" as he is listed in the boxscore, hits for the pitcher or for those who enter the game in relief of the pitcher. The pitcher is not required to leave the game, as he was when a pinch-hitter batted for him.

"No matter how hard you try," Casey Stengel once said, "there ain't no place in the batting order where you can hide the pitcher. He's still gonna come to bat when you least want him to." The designated hitter changed that; it did, indeed, make it possible to "hide" the pitcher.

To understand why the American League voted for the rule, all one had to do was look at team financial statements for the previous year. Eight of the twelve teams in the league lost money. Owners wanted to do something to increase run production, to make games more exciting, and the designated hitter was their solution. The more successful National League decided to watch and wait before trying it.

The designated hitter really wasn't new. It had been proposed to the major league rules committee in 1929. The International League gave the idea a try in 1969. More home runs were struck, more runs were scored, and team batting averages rose by as much as 17 points.

Once the American League voted the rule into existence, it aroused much comment, pro and con. Those who favored the rule said the immediate effect would be to perk up the game. Instead of having to watch a pitcher bat, most of whom were wholly inept at the plate, fans would get to see a "big man."

The rule was also expected to please the fans in that it would prolong the careers of aging superstars, men like Tony Oliva, Frank Howard, Orlando Cepeda, and Harmon Killebrew. As designated hitters, these men would merely have to swing a bat and run the bases; they would never have to play the field and suffer the resultant fatigue.

Pitchers, starting pitchers, would benefit, too, it was argued. In a close game, when a run was needed, managers would be far less likely to yank the starting pitcher. There would be no reason to, so long as the man was pitching well.

Yanks' Ron Blomberg (right, pictured with coach Elston Howard) was first designated hitter in baseball history. His bat was sent to Cooperstown for display in the Hall of Fame.

Among those who looked with disfavor on the designated hitter rule were those American League pitchers who also happened to be good hitters. Take Jim Palmer of the Baltimore Orioles, for instance. Palmer could bunt well and he hit the long ball occasionally. His average was always above .200. Since only a small handful of pitchers in the league hit as well as Palmer, the Orioles had a distinct advantage over the opposing team whenever he was in the lineup. But under the conditions of the designated hitter rule, Palmer's advantage was canceled out.

Most of these who opposed the rule, however, did so on the basis of tradition. It was said that the rulesmakers were upsetting the delicate subtleties of the hitter-pitcher relationship, and thus rendering serious damage. Traditionalists called the new rule "a cheap gimmick."

Whatever the pros and cons, hitters agree it is more difficult to be a designated hitter than a plain, ordinary pinch-hitter. The designated hitter has to make himself bear down four or five times in an afternoon, and this is the heart of the problem. Since he doesn't play the field, he has very little to occupy himself in between his appearances at the plate. So he tries to stay active, to keep alert. He

Designated hitter rule works to the disadvantage of good-hitting pitchers such as Jim Palmer.

studies the pitcher and talks to the team's other hitters. Some designated hitters take practice swings in the clubhouse while the other team is at bat.

Gates Brown was frequently used as a designated hitter during 1973. Which was easier, pinch-hitting or designated hitting? "When you're a designated hitter," he said, "you're looser, you swing away. If you don't get a hit the first or second time, you've still got a couple of more chances.

"Pinch-hitting is tougher. You get only one shot. You just try to make contact."

It is generally agreed that designated hitters have added color to games, but as far as increasing run production is concerned, their influence has been only barely noticeable. A survey conducted by *The New York Times* during the 1973 season showed that the American League teams were averaging 7.32 runs a game (for both teams). According to the report, that put "the runs per game right back where they had been two years ago." The *Times* added: "This is a staggeringly modest achievement for so radical a change."

It may not be the rule that is at fault. Perhaps it's the quality and character of the batters, their inability to deal with the unique pressures of the pinch-hitter's role. Smokey Burgess, where are you?

SUPERHITTERS

One of the nicest tributes Chicago's Dick Allen ever received came during the final game of the 1972 season. The White Sox had been eliminated from the pennant race and there were only four or five thousand people in the stands. Dick came to bat in the ninth inning and struck out. As he made his way to the dugout, the fans rose as one and started clapping and cheering. They were simply saying "thank you" to Allen for all that he had done with his bat that year.

Allen, at 5-foot-10, 187 pounds, doesn't compare in size to Frank Howard, Harmon Killebrew, or some of the other noted sluggers of the day. Yet Allen hits with all the power of a man who is fifty or more pounds heavier. Like all of the better hitters, he's able to delay his swing until the last instant, then lash the bat around with incredible speed. What's notable about Allen is that he does his lashing with a bat that weighs 40 ounces, almost half a pound heavier than the bat used by other hitters his size.

Allen has broad shoulders, powerful biceps, and thick wrists. Combine these endowments with the 40-ounce bat he swings and the result is some extraordinary accomplishment. Several times he's belted homers that have traveled 500 to 565 feet. He once hit a home run at the White Sox home grounds that sailed over the 50-foot scoreboard

Until he joined the White Sox, Allen seldom had reason to grin.

that is 408 feet from home plate. At Yankee Stadium, where stone memorials to Babe Ruth and other heroes once stood near the centerfield wall, a group of fans once unfurled a banner that read: SAVE OUR MONUMENTS; WALK ALLEN.

As the most electrifying player in the history of the White Sox, Dick Allen ranks as one of baseball's superstars. What qualities make some players superior to all others? You have to be able to hit, hit with power, run, throw, and field. Allen qualifies on each count.

It is difficult to imagine the broad-shouldered Allen, who was voted Most Valuable Player in the American League in 1972, ever being not wanted. But it happened—several times.

Dick Allen grew up in Wampum, Pennsylvania —population, 1,090—as one of nine children raised by a widowed mother. It was a close-knit family, and when Dick signed his first professional contract in 1959, receiving a bonus of $60,000, he used almost half of it to buy a new home for his mother.

While it was baseball dollars that helped to lead the family out of poverty, the Allens were better known for basketball. Three of Dick's brothers won all-state honors in the sport, and he followed in that tradition. Though only 5-foot-10 as a senior, he could stuff the ball, backward as well as forward. The team won the state championship twice during Dick's high school years. He was offered more than a dozen college scholarships, but the money put up by the Phillies was a far greater lure.

Dick's early baseball years were not always happy ones. He was eighteen, shy and unsure of himself, when he joined the Phillies in the spring of 1960 at their training base in Clearwater, Florida. He got a shock at the local airport when he found there were separate facilities for blacks and whites. "It confused and frightened me," he was to say later. The roommate the Phillies assigned to him didn't help matters. He was Marcelino Lopez, a Cuban pitcher. He didn't speak any English and Dick spoke no Spanish.

The Phillies sent Allen to Elmira of the New York–Penn League, where he batted .281 but had an atrocious time in the field, topping all shortstops in errors with 48. It was often a lonely year for him, and he accrued $400 in telephone tolls in calls to his mother and brothers.

A year at Twin Falls in the Pioneer League followed. Now at second base, Allen continued to have his problems with ground balls, but began to display the power which later would become his hallmark, hitting 21 home runs and driving in 94 runs. His average was .317.

After a year at Williamsport in the Eastern League, where he boosted his batting average to .329, Allen was promoted to Little Rock in the International League. The Phillies neglected to tell Allen that he was to be the team's first black player, and so he was wholly unprepared for the heckling, the crank telephone calls he received, and the signs in the stands that read: GO HOME, NIGGER. "It was like I was playing baseball in prison," he once said of the experience. "I couldn't go here; I couldn't go

Dick Allen uses a heavy 40-ounce bat, has a powerful swing.

there. It was as if I wasn't a human being." More than once that season Dick thought about abandoning his career, but his mother kept telling him, "Don't quit." Eventually, Allen overcame. He ended the season with a .297 average, 33 home runs, and the Little Rock fans voted him the team's "Most Popular Player" award.

Now the Phillies were ready to give him a try in the big time, but first they had to find a place for him to play. During his four years in the minors, Allen had played in the outfield, at shortstop, second base, and first base. The Phillies put him at third base. He had many difficult moments there that season, leading the league in errors for third basemen with 41, and he also was the league leader in strikeouts. But he connected frequently and when he did the results were often noteworthy. He batted .318, with 29 homers, and scored a league-leading 125 runs. He was an easy winner in the Rookie of the Year balloting.

But it was not a season that Allen looks back upon happily. The Philadelphia fans seemed never to have noticed what he did with his bat; instead, they booed him for his errors. When the team went into a slump in the final two weeks of the season, and promptly blew the pennant, Allen seemed to be held personally responsible for the collapse.

Things kept getting worse. The next season Allen got into a fight with teammate Frank Thomas, the two trading punches near the batting

Now a first baseman, Allen has played third, second, and shortstop.

cage before a game. Thomas happened to be a favorite of the Phillie fans and when, shortly after the fracas, he was traded away, Allen was blamed. The boos and catcalls became louder and more frequent.

Allen's career almost came to an abrupt end in 1967. He was trying to push his stalled automobile when a headlight shattered and one hand was slashed by the shards of glass. The injury sidelined him for the final month of the season. Although he hit 33 home runs the next season, his average slipped to .263 from a career high of .318. The hand was partly responsible. Even today, he feels it's only 90 per cent effective.

The accident added to Allen's woes, being taken as evidence that he was "trouble." There were rumors that he enjoyed strong drink and stayed out all night. In his final year with the Phillies, he had several run-ins with manager Gene Mauch. Allen was fined heavily as part of Mauch's plan for reforming him. When Allen rebelled against Mauch's rigid system of discipline by leaving the club, he was suspended. Allen returned to the lineup in July that season, but only after extracting a promise from Philadelphia owner Bob Carpenter that he would be traded at the end of the year.

When Allen's name was announced over the P.A. system for the first time following the suspension, the "boo birds" raised the roof. Other players have been booed; other players have been hooted at. But for Allen it had been going on for years—six of them. The vocal criticism was bad enough, but he was often a target for assorted pieces of debris, so often, in fact, that he got into the habit of putting on his batting helmet whenever he went out onto the field.

Philadelphia did trade him—to St. Louis. And so the merry-go-round began, stopping once a year. The stops—besides St. Louis—were Los Angeles and Chicago.

With each club, Allen quickly established two things: he could hit a baseball, hit it hard and hit it far, but he wanted to be able to hit it under his own set of ground rules. Mel Durslag, a West Coast sports columnist, described Allen aptly when he said he was "a nonconformist romping through a sport whose basic premise is conformity."

Allen thought about quitting after the Dodgers traded him. "It seemed nobody really wanted me," he told sportswriter Milt Gross. "They just wanted to use me. I was a piece of property they shifted from city to city." But Allen talked to his mother, who told him, "Listen, son, go help Chuck out."

Chuck was Chuck Tanner, manager of the White Sox. Tanner had grownup in New Castle, Pennsylvania, just ten miles north of Wampum. He had competed against the oldest of the Allen boys, Coy, in high school basketball. Tanner knew what Allen was capable of doing.

Tanner had a different philosophy than other managers Allen had played for. "There is no hard line here," Tanner said. "Everybody is different. There are 25 different rules for 25 different players." If Allen missed infield practice, it didn't matter. If he didn't show up for batting practice, so be it. All he had to do was be on the field when the first pitch was thrown.

What happened is well known. Allen hit a home run in his first game for the White Sox, and he doubled home the tie-breaking run in the second game. At the end of the team's first road trip, he was hitting a hefty .417. He received more votes in the All Star balloting than any other player.

Allen came to be well-liked by his Chicago teammates. When a hitter was having problems Allen would talk to the man and try to help him. A newspaper reporter discovered Allen taking batting practice at 7 o'clock one morning. "Don't write about it," said Allen with a grin. "People will say I'm just getting in."

The fans came to regard Allen as a folk hero and flocked to the ancient White Sox park to see him. Attendance for the season increased by more than 350,000 over the previous year.

Thanks to Allen's robust hitting, Chicago remained in the pennant race until the last weeks of the season. "The main thing with the White Sox is Dick Allen," said Oakland pitcher Blue Moon

A frequent sight at White Sox Stadium: Allen (15) being congratulated by teammates following home run blast.

Odom. "If you can get him out, you can control the game."

Allen stands a bit deeper in the batter's box than normal. He sets his feet about as far apart as the width of his shoulders. He takes a full stride.

He makes a particular effort to keep his eyes level. If the hitter tilts his head, Allen says, his ability to see the pitcher and pitch has to be reduced.

Allen realizes that pitchers often try to get him out by jamming him, by pitching close to his hands. So he works on hitting pitches that break in on him, and he's had some success in slicing hits to the "wrong" field—right field, in his case.

Allen slugged a league-leading 37 home runs in 1972, batted in 113 runs, and ended with a .308 average. When they counted up the ballots in the voting for the league's Most Valuable Player, Allen was the winner in a landslide. "I hope I'm actually worthy of the honor," said Allen, then added, "I've had everything from baseball, except the joy of playing on a winner." He pledged himself to working toward that goal.

While Dick Allen has ranked as the most dangerous slugger in the American League in recent years, over in the National League that billing has gone to St. Louis' Joe Torre, winner of that league's MVP award in 1971. It was a remarkable year for the versatile Torre, who has played first and third base and caught. He hit .363, driving in 137 runs and collecting 230 hits and 24 homers. A right-handed batter, he averaged a remarkable .363 against right-handed pitchers, and .362 against lefties.

Torre broke into major league baseball with the Milwaukee Braves in 1961 and went to the Cards eight years later in exchange for Orlando Cepeda. During Torre's years with the Braves, the team always had Hank Aaron, and when he joined the Cards there were such players as Dick Allen, Lou Brock, and Curt Flood in the lineup. "The pressure was never on me," he once remarked. "Not until the Cards traded Dick Allen. That's when the team started looking to me.

"It wasn't so much pressure as it was responsibility. I rooted and hollered more than I ever had before because I didn't want anyone to get down on themselves or the team."

While his leadership qualities were important, it was his bat that boosted the Cards into a second-place finish. Not only did he hit for average, but he hit when it counted, driving in 22 game-winning runs. St. Louis fans agree he's the best all-around batter the Cards have had since the glory days of Stan Musial.

Torre is 6-foot-1, 205 pounds. His dark hair, heavy brows, and swarthy face give him a menacing appearance. He was born in Brooklyn and grew up there, playing sandlot baseball as his two older brothers had. Brother Frank, a first baseman, showed the way. After three years in the minors, he moved up to the Milwaukee Braves, and that was the goal that his kid brother set for himself.

Young Joe started out playing third base, but he had so much difficulty keeping his weight under control that he switched to catching. While there was some question as to where he might play, no one had any doubts about his ability to hit the ball. Milwaukee gave him a $26,000 bonus to sign. After a year with Eau Claire in the Northern League and part of a year with Louisville in the American Association, Joe moved up to the Braves. In his first year with the team, he hit .278 in 113 games, belted 10 home runs, and finished second to the Cubs' Billy Williams in the Rookie-of-the-Year voting.

Torre displays powerful follow-through.

For four consecutive years, beginning in 1964, Torre was the National League's All-Star catcher. The Braves' pitchers lauded him for his intelligence, strength, and durability. He hit as high as .321.

But he had problem years with the Braves. Injuries hampered him in 1967, and 1968 was worse. On the opening day of the season, a foul tip split one of his fingers and he was sidelined for several days. He returned to the lineup for a night game against Chicago. Hank Aaron was on first when Torre came to bat. As the pitch came in, Torre shot a glance toward Aaron to see whether he was running. He shouldn't have. When he looked back for the ball, he couldn't find it and it slammed into his cheekbone, crunching three bones in the roof of his mouth.

It was many weeks before his vision returned to normal, but many months before his hitting did. "I was gun-shy at the plate," he recalls. His batting average for the season fell to .271, lowest ever for him. He hit only 10 home runs and drove in only 55 runs. The fact that he wasn't hitting was bad enough. Worse, he was feuding with Atlanta manager Paul Richards. Richards vowed he would trade him and Torre ended up with the Cardinals as a result.

In his first weeks with St. Louis, Torre found himself still shying away from inside pitches. Some advice he got from Frank Robinson helped to

Torre is glum after striking out.

restore his confidence. Robinson told him that it had once taken him a year to get over being struck by a pitch. "It meant a lot to hear that," Torre said. "I no longer felt like there was something wrong with me."

Torre went on to have a fine season, batting .289, driving in 101 runs. Before the next season began, then nearing thirty, he took a close look at himself. He realized that he was carrying around a great deal of extra weight and it was time to do something about it. "I wasn't too concerned about the weight hurting my hitting," he said, "but I wondered how much longer I could go on catching. Surely, not more than two or three years."

So Torre went on a strict diet. It called for eight glasses of water a day, plenty of lean steaks, cottage cheese, eggs (but not fried eggs), and salads. He lost 12 pounds in two weeks and continued to lose small amounts gradually. As his weight went down, his batting average went up. Torre hit .325 that year, best ever for him, but only a prelude to his MVP season.

Torre's plan to lose weight combined nicely with manager Red Schoendienst's wish to have him take over at third base. He could never have played the position if he hadn't trimmed down.

At the end of 1972, Torre could boast a lifetime batting average of .303. Only a small handful of National Leaguers—Hank Aaron, Pete Rose, Willie

Mays, and Manny Sanguillen—were higher on the list. One reason Torre does so well is that he is seldom bothered by prolonged slumps. He says he's able to avoid slumps by always trying to be mentally ready when stepping up to hit. "You can't do what a lot of young players do when you begin to slacken off," he says. "You can't change bats over and over and change your stance and move around in the batter's box. You can't panic when you're in a slump."

Two or three times a week Joe talks to his brother Frank about his hitting. Frank usually has this advice: "Don't go for home runs."

Torre's homer total after twelve years in the majors was a modest 216, but it could have been greater, far greater, if he had allowed himself to become a pull hitter. "I've always tried to avoid this. I say hit the ball hard somewhere, don't try to guide it," he once told John Davaney of *Sport* Magazine. "Go into the ball, don't try to pull it.

"To me it's a lot harder to hit a single when a man is on second base than it is to hit a home run with no one on base. With a man in scoring position, a pitcher is more careful. With no one on, he's likely to be more careless."

Not only does Torre aid the Cards with his consistent hitting, but he is also the acknowledged leader of the team. If he goes four for four and the Cards lose, he broods. But winning puts a smile on

The team leader, Torre has a word of encouragement for Scipio Spinks.

his face, even if he's gone zero for four. During a game, the Cardinal pitcher often relies on Torre for advice, calling him over from his station at third base to ask him how to pitch to a certain hitter. "The catcher here [Ted Simmons] is young," Torre points out, "and he's been very good at taking suggestions from me." Torre has also been able to help pitchers by spotting flaws in their delivery.

Someone once asked Torre, what makes a superstar? "That's easy," he answered, grinning, "It's any player who earns more than $100,000 a year." Torre himself qualifies on that basis. So does Dick Allen. In fact, early in 1973, Allen signed a three-year contract estimated to be worth $675,000. It was, at the time, the biggest contract in baseball history.

Pete Rose is another player whose annual paychecks add up to $100,000 plus. But Rose has entered the exclusive circle largely because he hits singles. Of course, he hits them oftener than anyone else in baseball.

Rose joined the Reds in 1963 and two years later became a .300 hitter. Since then he's been an incredibly consistent performer. Each year Rose's goal is to collect at least 200 hits, and when he doesn't reach that level it's news. His career goal is nine 200-hit seasons, a feat achieved only by Ty Cobb. As of 1973, Rose needed only four more

Cincinnati superstar Pete Rose.

96

seasons with 200 hits to equal Cobb's mark.

To get 200 hits in a season is a formidable task. You have to play in virtually every game. You need several hot hitting streaks and you can't allow yourself to fall into a long slump at any point.

Getting hits and getting on base is what the Reds want Rose to do. Other players in the Cincinnati lineup—notably Tony Perez and Johnny Bench—provide the punch. Bench, of course, ranks as one of the game's superhitters, too. He won his second Most Valuable Player award in 1972 at the age of twenty-four, and thus stands as the youngest player ever to win two MVP awards. (Bench is profiled in a companion volume to this book entitled *Pitchers and Pitching*, Dodd, Mead, 1972.)

"I'd like to get 3,000 hits for my career," says Rose. After he had passed the 2,000-hit mark in 1973, he noted that he was the only active player with a possible chance of getting *4,000 hits.* "That would be an untouchable record," he says.

Rose, a self-taught switch-hitter, has more power from the left side. But he is about equally proficient at handling right- or left-handed pitching, as a comparison of his batting average against each shows.

Rose is quick to admit that being a switch-hitter gives him an important edge. "Those sliders and curves are always coming in, not going away," he says, and when he says it he usually grins.

Rose likes to hit the ball up the middle, although he was a major leaguer before he came to realize the advantage of this strategy. In 1968, Rose broke his thumb and had to watch games from the press-box while the injury healed. "It was then I realized how big the opening was up the middle," he says. "It doesn't look so big when you're at the plate because you've got the pitcher standing in front of you."

Rose usually gets off to a slow start, hitting in the 280s during April and May. But warm weather heats him up, and there have been seasons where he has hit over .400 in July and August. "I prefer to play when it's hot," he says, "Sometimes I have a problem getting loosened up in the spring. I like to play in a T-shirt. I like to sweat when I'm playing."

Rose is not without power as a hitter. In the 1972 World Series against Oakland, he blasted two important home runs. Twice he has hit 16 homers for the season. "If Pete wanted to go for home runs," says Sparky Anderson, the Reds' manager, "he could hit 25 a season. But it would be the worst thing he could do."

Rose is well known in Cincinnati. He was born there—in 1942—and grew up just a few miles from where Riverfront Stadium is now located. His father, Pete Rose, Sr., played halfback for a local semipro team and also boxed professionally. Pete's brother Dave was a good enough ball player to rate a major league try. Pete himself never attracted much attention as a high school player because he was too small, weighing only 155 pounds. But he had an uncle, a scout for the Reds, who was able to convince club officials that, given time, Pete would develop in size and strength. He was proven right, of course, for today Pete stands 5-foot-10 and weighs 185.

Pete signed his first contract in June, 1960, a few days after he had graduated from high school. He received a $1,200 bonus. After a year at Geneva in the New York–Pennsylvania League, Pete was promoted to Tampa in the Florida State League where he hit .331. Cincinnati officials needed no further convincing and the following year he was wearing

It's Rose's job to get on base. Others in the Reds' lineup have the power to drive him home.

a Reds' uniform.

Rose hit only .273 in his first year in the major leagues but he still managed to win Rookie-of-the-Year honors. What impressed everyone was the young man's boundless energy and enthusiasm.

Indeed, hustle characterizes everything that Rose does on the playing field. He runs to first base on walks. He runs out to pick up his glove. Any time he hits the ball, he breaks for first base like a man being chased by a mugger. He stretches singles into doubles, and doubles into triples. Headfirst slides are his trademark.

Take what happened in the 1970 All-Star Game. Play was in the bottom of the twelfth inning. Rose was perched on second base. Pitcher Clyde Wright yielded a single and Rose took off, careening around third base and down the line. Catcher Ray Fosse was set to receive the ball when suddenly Rose slammed into him, sending Fosse in one direction and the ball in another and giving the National League a controversial win. "I think he could have gone around me," Fosse said later, and several of his teammates agreed. "No way," said Rose in his defense. "He was a full step up the line. I had to hit him." One thing everyone agreed on; the block could have won Rose a starting job with the Green Bay Packers.

Most fans recall that play first whenever Rose's name is mentioned. He himself, however, has more

Rose, crouching, awaits the pitch.

99

vivid memories of other games. One took place in 1968, when Rose was dueling Matty Alou, then with the Pittsburgh Pirates, for the National League batting title. Rose, hit by a late-in-the-season slump, watched his lead over Alou melt away. With two games to play, the two men were in a virtual tie.

In the next to the last game of the season, Rose faced Gaylord Perry, who was then with the San Francisco Giants. Rose got four straight hits off Perry. ("All on spitballs," he once recalled.) He was standing on first base after the first hit, when Perry yelled over to him. "Got enough?" he asked.

"I'll take one more," Rose shouted back.

When Rose came up to bat for the fifth time, catcher Dick Dietz spoke to him. "Perry wants to know what kind of a pitch you'd like him to throw to you," said Dietz.

Rose paid no attention to the query. When Perry threw a fastball, Pete slammed it for a double, which made him 5-for-5 for the day.

Alou managed to keep pace with 4-for-4 for the afternoon. But on the last day of the season, Rose got a double in three at-bats while Alou went hitless. Pete finished the season with a .335 average, three points ahead of Alou.

The very next season, 1969, Rose again went down to the wire in the batting race. This time Roberto Clemente furnished the opposition.

Rose had a narrow lead on the final day of the season. Before the game, he figured out that if he went 0-for-4 and Clemente went 4-for-4, the batting title would go to Clemente.

Rose failed in his first three attempts. Then he was given the news that Clemente, at that point, was 3-for-3. "When I came to bat the fourth time, I was really sweating," Rose recalls. "I figured the last thing anybody would be expecting was a bunt, so I laid it down.

"I never ran faster to first base. I doubt any record-breaking sprinter could have beaten me. When I crossed the base I was safe, and I knew I had my second straight batting championship."

Pete's teammates recognize that he is one of the game's foremost competitors. They've nicknamed him "Charlie Hustle" and they also call him "Mr. Perpetual Motion."

"I couldn't believe the guy when I joined the club," says Woody Woodward, a former Cincinnati infielder. "He's the same off the field as on—go, go, go. On the team bus going to the ballpark, he can't sit still. He walks up and down the aisle or stands by the door waiting to get out."

In his desire to make Cincinnati a winning team, Rose has done everything but hawk soft drinks in the stands. He has shifted from the infield to the outfield, and there he has won respect for his rifle arm, consistently ranking at the top of league or near the top in assists. He has even led the team in getting hit by the pitch.

Rose has never had to force himself to hustle, however. "I love to play baseball," he says. "It isn't just a job with me. When it's fun, that's the way you play, with hustle."

Rose's goal is to manage the Reds one day. But on the basis of his drive and enthusiasm as a player, and the way he continues to punch out base hits, it will be many years before he's ready to realize that ambition.

CHASING A MYTH

"It is a matter of history now that Ruth increased his home run output for a season to a record 60 in 1927 and hit 714 of them in his career. As common as home runs are today, it is at least doubtful that any player will ever top that total. To do it a batter would have to average 35 or more for twenty years, and although some of them have maintained such a pace for ten seasons, to keep it up for another ten has been beyond their powers. Perhaps some day there will be another Ruth, but he will have to be seen to be believed."

Kings of the Diamond (1965)
by Lee Allen and Tom Meany

Babe Ruth was more than a home run hitter. He was a folk hero, a superman, Babe, the Bambino, the Sultan of Swat.

To break a record of Ruth's was one thing; displacing him in the public's mind was something else. Roger Maris found this out when he hit 61 home runs in 1961, exceeding Ruth's season total by one. It was brought home to Hank Aaron the moment he began to menace Ruth's lifetime home run total, that magic number, 714.

Aaron himself realized the realities of the situa-

Ruth grabbed the bat at the handle end, swung from the heels.

tion. Once asked what it would mean if he hit *750* home runs, he said, "Ruth's home runs are always going to be a legend. No matter who comes along and hits more, people are not going to accept the fact that someone is capable of breaking his record.

"If I hit 750 home runs, it would just be that I hit 750 home runs. That's all. That's all."

Much of what has been written about Babe Ruth's boyhood bears little relationship to objective truth. But thanks to meticulous research done by James H. Bready of the Baltimore *Sun*, it is known that Ruth was born at the home of his maternal grandfather on Emory Street in Baltimore on February 6, 1895. When he was seven, Ruth was admitted to St. Mary's Industrial Home for Boys in Baltimore, a refuge for orphaned children and those from broken homes. He was in and out of St. Mary's several times over the next ten years. Ruth's mother died when he was seventeen.

Ruth learned the tailoring trade at St. Mary's and also some baseball. He was a left-handed catcher, highly regarded for his strong and accurate arm.

One Jack Dunn, who owned the Baltimore Orioles, then members of the International League, visited St. Mary's in February, 1914, became Ruth's legal guardian, and signed him to an Oriole contract. Ruth joined the team at training camp in Fayetteville, North Carolina, in the spring of 1914. Like any young rookie, Ruth was often the butt of jokes and pranks. One day before the opening of the season, Sam Steinman, a coach, spoke to the veteran players, warning them, "You'd better be careful; that kid's one of Jack Dunn's babes." According to many history books, that is how George Herman Ruth got his nickname.

When the Baltimore team needed cash, they sold Ruth's contract to the Boston Red Sox. The following year, 1915, Ruth earned a job as a starting pitcher, finishing the season with an 18–6 record. Frequently used as a pinch-hitter, he batted .315 and struck four home runs, one of which gave a hint of things to come. It boomed off his bat one July afternoon in St. Louis, and caused the Boston *Herald* to comment: "The home run cleared the right field bleachers and landed miles and miles away in the midst of a throbbing brewery district. It was the longest hit recorded at the local grounds since they were built. Others have cleared the fence but had neither the speed nor the height of Ruth's Homeric swat today."

Ruth was switched to the outfield on a full-time basis in 1919 and hit 29 home runs. The next year Ruth's contract was sold to the New York Yankees for $100,000, which gave his career a big boost. Playing in New York, the nation's communications center, headquarters for the wire services, national magazines, book publishing, and the radio (and later, television) networks has always been an enormous benefit to the professional athlete, and

Ruth in 1929

said the *Literary Digest* in 1921. "He has not only slugged his way to fame but he has got everybody else doing it. The home run fever is in the air.

"Babe not only smashed all records, he has smashed the long accepted system of things in the batting world, and on the ruins of that system he has erected another system, or rather lack of system, whose dominant quality is brute force."

Choke-hitting, which meant shortening one's grip on the bat, was what the *Literary Digest* was referring to when it used the term "long accepted system." The great Ty Cobb, who was in his prime when Ruth broke in, was a choke hitter. So was Eddie Collins, who was to attain a lifetime batting average of .333. Young players copied Cobb and Collins.

Then came Babe Ruth, swinging from the heels. "Some folks say I was responsible for the development of 'swing hitting,' Ruth said in his autobiography. "Maybe," he added, "they're right."

Statistics bore out that Ruth's method was the best method. Before the Babe, the record for career home runs was held by Clifford (Gavvy) Cravath, who spent most of his 13-year stay in the major leagues with the Phillies. At the time of his retirement in 1920, Cravath had 119 homers. Ruth surpassed that total in 1921, a year he hit 59, jumping his lifetime total to 162. And Ruth was only twenty-six, with a decade of big hitting ahead of him.

Ruth was tall, 6-foot-2. He had long arms, thick

this was especially true in Ruth's case. When, in 1920, his home run total came to 54, and the following year when he increased it to 59, news of these heroic achievements was flashed far and wide.

"He has batted home runs at so dizzy a pace that he has fired the enthusiasm of the entire country," wrists, and heavy hands. In his later years with the Yanks, his disregard for training rules was evidenced by the extra poundage he carried, concentrated around his middle. His spindly legs seemed too fragile to support it all.

A left-handed batter, Ruth would stand with his feet close together, his body erect, and his bat tilted over his shoulder. He peered at the pitcher solemnly. If the ball was to his liking, he took a murderous swing. The fans often cheered when he struck out swinging, for they could see he was doing all that was physically possible to drive one out.

It is often overlooked, but Ruth's baseball talents were not limited to what he could do with the bat. His teammates and players who opposed him knew that he had a powerful throwing arm and had unerring judgment as to which base to throw to. He made many spectacular catches up against the bleacher wall in Yankee Stadium's right field. As a base runner, he had determination and good speed.

Ruth was seldom less than an exciting figure, whether on the field or off. He dressed sportily and ate and drank what he liked, and he liked everything. During a game, he would gulp down soft drinks almost as quickly as they could be provided.

Ruth's slugging not only brought him fame, but started baseball trend that has lasted to this day.

Ruth and Lou Gehrig

Soft drinks were not all he drank, of course. He enjoyed the bright lights, the crowds, the music, and he enjoyed them with such regularity that he was in frequent conflict with Yankee manager Miller Huggins.

Once Huggins fined Ruth $1,000 for staying out all night, but withdrew the punishment when Ruth promised to behave. Of course, he didn't. Ultimately Ruth's flaunting of the rules began to show up in his batting average and the team went into a slump. Huggins could take it no more. He suddenly suspended Ruth and fined him $5,000 for "misconduct." Ruth was enraged and lashed out at Huggins to the press, but in the end he apologized to the manager and his abuse of the rules became less flagrant.

Ruth was never pictured on a box of breakfast cereal nor did he ever do a razor blade commercial, but he found plenty of ways to add to his income and keep his name before the public. He endorsed cigarettes and had his own brand of cigars. His name appeared on candy bars (and still does) and sports equipment. Books and newspaper articles on how to play baseball were written under his name, and he appeared on radio programs and made a motion picture film.

In the years that Ruth hit the most home runs, he had few competitors. When, in 1927, the year he struck his record 60, Ruth's output represented more than 12 per cent of the American League's home run production. To attain that percentage today, a player would have to hit 120 home runs.

The salary that Ruth received also helped to make him a bigger-than-life figure. In 1930 and again in 1931, the Yankees paid Ruth $80,000, truly an enormous sum for the time. These were depression days in the United States, and falling prices and unemployment were rife. Even the President wasn't paid as much as Ruth.

Ruth provided one of the most unforgettable moments in baseball history during a World Series game in 1932 against the Chicago Cubs. Facing the Cubs' Charlie Root, Ruth pointed to the bleachers, indicating he meant to hit the ball there —and then he did. Three years later his career ended, fittingly in headline fashion. Ruth had been released by the Yankees and had caught on with the Boston Braves. The team was at Forbes Field to play the Pirates. Babe belted the ball out of the park three times that afternoon, his last great performance.

Ruth died of cancer in 1948, but well before his death his impact upon baseball was easy to perceive. Almost single-handedly Ruth demonstrated the value of the home run, not only its tactical importance, but how it could be used to lure customers through the turnstiles. As a result of Ruth, club owners began to design their stadiums to make the home run a more frequent occurrence, and hitters everywhere, starting with the very

youngest, were holding the bat down at the end and swinging for all they were worth.

To the general public, Ruth was more myth than man. When Jimmy Foxx threatened Ruth's home run record in 1932, and when Hank Greenberg did in 1938, both received their share of "hate mail" from those who felt they were not worthy of wearing Ruth's mantle. The same thing happened to Ralph Kiner in 1949, the year he hit 54 home runs.

When Roger Maris managed to surpass Ruth, the baseball establishment treated him shabbily. Commissioner Ford C. Frick declared that Maris' 61 would have to be accompanied by an asterisk in the record book, which called attention to the fact that he played a 162-game season. The season was 154 games in length in Ruth's day. Yet Maris' record was a "season" record. Why should the number of games played have any significance? The answer is, they shouldn't have.

Rogers Hornsby commented that it was a shame that Ruth's record had to be broken "by a .269 hitter." All in all, Maris was embittered by the treatment. He would not attend Old-Timers' Day celebrations or make personal appearances that had anything to do with baseball.

There is very little that is similar in the careers of Babe Ruth and Hank Aaron. The times were different. Baseball was a much different sport. The nation was in a jubilant mood in the 1920s, having wound up a big war in 1918, and it was a time for celebrating, for drinking and dancing, for fast automobiles and stock market gambling. Baseball was a much different sport.

The personalities of Ruth and Aaron were very different. There was a world of difference in their backgrounds. Born in Mobile, Alabama, on February 3, 1934, the third of eight children, Aaron grew up in a baseball-minded family. His father and uncle were well-known local players, and Hank and two of his brothers inherited their skills. Brother Tommy was later to be Hank's teammate on the Braves.

"I was a lazy and smart kid," Hank once said, "lazy when it came to doing chores around the house, but smart when it came to baseball and other sports. This is what I really wanted to do, even when I was eleven and twelve years old."

His high school had no baseball team so young Hank played on weekends in a league organized by the local recreation department. Later he joined a team known as the Mobile Black Bears. One day the Bears played an exhibition game against the barnstorming Indianapolis Clowns of the Negro American League. Hank made a vivid impression on the pros and the next spring they offered him a contract. Hank, a high school senior at the time, jumped at the chance. The salary of $200 a month was too much to turn down.

Once he broke into the starting lineup, hits ripped off Aaron's bat with startling frequency. One

Aaron's wrists were always incredibly quick and powerful.

afternoon in a doubleheader against the Kansas City Monarchs, he got ten hits in eleven trips to the plate. He led the league in hitting with a .467 average and major league scouts began to take notice.

Two teams were particularly interested in him, the San Francisco Giants and the Braves, who were then based in Milwaukee. The Braves offered Hank $350 a month if he would sign; the Giants offered $200 a month less. This made it an easy choice for eighteen-year-old Henry.

The Braves paid the Indianapolis Clowns $10,000 for Hank's contract. The club regarded him as an outstanding prospect, even though he batted cross-handed, that is, he placed his left hand above his right when he gripped the bat. While this unorthodox style probably cost him ten or twenty points on his batting average, he feels it has had value. "I think it had a lot to do with the development of my wrists," he once said, "because you really had to be quick." Aaron's wrists were not only very quick, they were also very strong. His sinewy forearms were another of his physical assets.

The late Dewey Griggs, a scout for the Braves, sought to correct Aaron's grip, instructing him to place the right hand above the left in accepted fashion. Although Aaron got three hits in the first game in which he used the right-above-left technique, it was more than a year before he felt com-

fortable with it. During his minor league career, when a pitcher got two strikes on him, he would often put his left hand back on top, hoping the manager wouldn't catch him.

It's unfortunate that someone didn't encourage Aaron to become a switch-hitter during the early stages of his baseball career. It would have been easy for him to learn, since he held the bat as a left-handed hitter does. All he would have had to do is cross over to the other side of the plate.

Aaron moved up the baseball ladder quickly. After a year at Eau Claire in the Northern League, he was promoted to Jacksonville, where he hit a league-leading .362. When the Braves' Bobby Thomson broke his leg in spring training in 1954, Hank got his chance.

Aaron had played shortstop and second base as a minor league player, and when the Braves switched him to the outfield he had his problems. He admitted in later years that he made "a lot of mistakes" as a rookie. But his teammates were very willing to overlook his fielding lapses because of the way he hit the ball. "He had the greatest hand action I had ever seen," Bobby Thomson once recalled, "a lethal way of whipping the bat around. And he hit nothing but line drives. Even on home runs, the ball jumped off his bat as if it had been fired from a cannon."

Aaron, however, didn't look like a slugger, nor was he built like one. A trim 180-pound, 6-footer,

Aaron swings and watches.

he gave the appearance of a singles hitter. People thought of him in terms of base hits and his batting average, not home runs. They did, that is, until the final years of his career.

Aaron was voted the National League's Most Valuable Player in 1957, a richly deserved honor. On September 22 that year, he hit his forty-second home run, and the Braves edged the Cardinals, 9–7, in ten innings. They needed one more victory to clinch the National League title.

The next night the Braves played the Cards at home before more than 40,000 fans. At the end of nine innings the score was tied, 2–2. In the bottom of the eleventh inning, Johnny Logan singled with one out, and the Braves had the potential pennant-winning run on first base. Eddie Mathews flied out. Up stepped Aaron. He had two hits already, one of which had contributed to a run.

The fans were on their feet and screaming. Bill Muffett went into his windup and fired a curve. Hank lashed at the ball, clouting it toward center field and the sign that read 402 feet. Wally Moon made a desperate leap. The ball passed over Moon's glove and disappeared beyond the fence. The Braves had won the pennant.

Aaron was mobbed by his teammates and carried from the field. The *Milwaukee Journal* described the feat in Biblical terms. "For Aaron stretched out his hand with his rod and smote the dust of the earth," said the paper, then added,

"Verily he did, and at 11:34 last night, he also smote a baseball over the center-field fence at County Stadium."

Aaron continued smiting the ball in the World Series, the Braves vs. the New York Yankees. He led both clubs in hitting (with a .393 average), in RBIs (with 7), and got at least one hit in each of the seven games, as the Braves turned back the Yankees.

In 1958, the Braves won the league crown again, but this time the Yankees took the World Series. In 1959 and again in 1969, the Braves were close, losing in play-off competition which would have led to the World Series.

Aaron took all of the adulation very much in stride. "Low-key" was the term often used to describe him. Yet Aaron was warm and sincere and people enjoyed meeting him. He would spend hours signing slips of paper for youthful autograph seekers and he seldom turned down a request for an interview.

But no one ever accused Aaron of flamboyance. He dressed stylishly but never in a way to attract attention. His off-the-field life seldom attracted the notice of the press.

In his quiet way, Aaron went about being merely superb. His wrist action at the plate was the envy of every player who has ever swung a bat at a thrown ball. He was so incredibly quick and powerful with his wrists that he was able to make up for any tech-

Aaron played first base in 1971, later returned to the outfield.

nical imperfections of his swing.

"Most people would never hit the ball the way I do," he said. "I have a hitch in my swing and I hit off my front foot. I've seen the movies. But my weight is forward and my hands are always back. Even when they throw me a change-up, I'm not out in front."

Ferguson Jenkins, a 20-game winner for the Cubs many times, once described what it was like to have to face Aaron: "Just when you think you've thrown the ball by him, he gets the bat around and hits it. Sometimes it seems like he takes the ball right out of the catcher's glove."

When Aaron was asked what quality made a superior hitter, he often replied with a one-word answer: "Aggressiveness." He described aggressiveness as "knowing what you want to do when you get to the plate, knowing what pitch you wanted to hit." Who, according to Aaron, were "aggressive" hitters? He named these: Stan Musial, Jackie Robinson, Frank Robinson, Ted Williams, and Willie Mays.

The Braves' franchise was switched from Milwaukee to Atlanta after the season of 1965, a change that helped Aaron. He called the climate in Atlanta "ideal." It was seldom cold, even early in the season. Atlanta Stadium was a help, too. It is 300 feet down each of the foul lines and 400 feet to dead center. The outfield fence is six feet in height. "If I hit a ball good," Aaron once observed, "it will go out, and it doesn't matter whether it's hit to right, left or center."

Aaron continued to play consistently excellent baseball, building his home run total year by year, but aside from his heroics in 1957, he seldom caused any great stir. He was known as a solid player, a complete player, and an artist with the bat, but other players—Willie Mays and Mickey Mantle, most notably—basked in the limelight. Then in 1968 Aaron went over the 500-homer mark, and people began to notice him.

After Aaron soared past 600 home runs, an

Aaron and Braves' manager Eddie Mathews.

Atlanta newspaperman asked Jimmy (the Greek) Snyder, the well-known Las Vegas bookmaker, to determine the odds on Aaron's chances of surpassing Babe Ruth's record of 714 home runs. Snyder said that Aaron had "an even chance." Aaron was then asked to comment on what Snyder had said. "If all goes well and I stay healthy," said Henry, "I think my chances are better than even." It was then that people *really* began to notice him.

As baseball entered the season of 1973, Aaron's home run total stood at 673 and he prepared himself for an all-out assault on Ruth's mark. By this time, Aaron had led the National League in every major batting category—hitting, home runs, and runs batted in—at least twice. Four times he had matched the number of his uniform—No. 44—in homers. His best output in each category was as follows: average, .355 (1959); home runs, 47 (1971); RBIs, 132 (1957). The record book gives evidence of Aaron's remarkable consistency. He has hit 30 or more home runs in each one of 15 seasons, a feat Babe Ruth accomplished "only" 13 times.

Aaron distinguished himself for more than just his ability to hit home runs. He has been one of two players in baseball history to total 3,000 hits *and* 500 homers. (Willie Mays was the other.) Aaron was one of five men to hit more than 30 homers in a season *and* steal more than 30 bases in the same season.

In 1973, Aaron went to bat for the 11,000th time. Only Ty Cobb, with 11,429 at-bats, remained ahead of Hank in that category. The same year, Aaron scored the 2,000th run of his career, a mark achieved by only three other players. And he became the pre-eminent right-hand hitter of all time later in the season when he topped Honus Wagner's record of 3,430 hits.

In the final stages of the attack upon the record, Aaron began holding the bat lower and closer to his body. He had found that swinging from a head-high angle, once normal for him, was the cause of nagging backaches. The new style caused him to pull the ball more.

Manager Eddie Mathews switched Aaron from right field into left field to lessen the strain on Henry's arm. The throws a right fielder must make, meant to keep a runner from advancing, are frequently longer than a left fielder's throws.

But if Aaron's skills diminished in the late stages of his career, you could never tell it from the way opposing teams regarded him. On one occasion Aaron was intentionally walked by the Cincinnati Reds late in a tie game with a man at third for the Braves. "I'm not going to let Hank Aaron beat me in that situation," said Cincinnati manager Sparky Anderson afterward. "I wouldn't care if he had retired and come down out of the stands to hit, I would have walked him. Aaron lives for those kind of situations."

Gene Mauch, manager of the Montreal Expos, has said this about Aaron, "We feel the same way about him as we did fifteen years ago. Any pitch above the belt is next-door to disaster."

Aging hitters see fastballs frequently because their reflexes have slipped. Willie Mays, in his last years in baseball, was often embarrassed by pitchers who zipped the ball right by him. Not so with Aaron. "Once in a while, when a pitcher thinks I might be tired, he might throw me a fastball," Aaron has said, "but I mostly see breaking stuff."

While opposing pitchers were causing Aaron no more than the usual amount of difficulty, the fans were becoming a problem, so much so that there were times that Aaron found it difficult to maintain his usual poise and serenity. The closer that Henry got to the record, the more letters and cards he received. They began pouring into the offices of the Atlanta Braves by the thousands each week. It wasn't the volume that upset Aaron. It was the fact that some of the mail contained racial slurs. "They call me 'nigger' and every other word you can imagine," Aaron said. "It bothers me."

The hometown fans in Atlanta did little to bolster Aaron's morale. Although Henry was an excellent drawing card on the road, in Atlanta people stayed away from the park in droves. And when

As pressure built, Aaron smiled less frequently.

enough fans turned out to make some noise, scattered boos could be heard. Early in 1973, Aaron had a run-in with a fan and threatened to go into the stands after him. "Most of the time the fans are fine," he said. "I don't care if they boo. They pay their money and they're entitled to that. But I just won't take it when it gets racial."

Why the "hate mail?" Why the boos? Of course, the color of Aaron's skin was part of the answer. The United States of the 1970s still had its share of bigots. Another factor was Aaron himself, his personality. The public wants its heroes to be more than technically perfect, more than consistently excellent. They want them to swagger. They want them to flaunt their skills. This was never Hank Aaron's way. But more than these things, there was the legendary quality of the name of Babe Ruth and the very sacredness of the number 714. It was a problem Aaron would never be able to solve. No one ever will.

HANK AARON'S MILESTONE HOME RUNS

No.   1—April 23, 1954, at St. Louis, off Vic Raschi
No. 100—August 15, 1957, at Cincinnati, off Don Gross
No. 200—July 3, 1960, at St. Louis, off Ron Kline
No. 300—April 19, 1963, at New York, off Roger Craig
No. 400—April 20, 1966, at Philadelphia, off Bo Belinsky
No. 500—July 14, 1968, at Atlanta, off Mike McCormick, San Francisco
No. 600—April 27, 1971, at Atlanta, off Gaylord Perry, San Francisco
No. 700—July 21, 1973, at Atlanta, off Ken Brett, Philadelphia
No. 713—September 29, 1973, at Atlanta, off Jerry Reuss, Houston
No. 714—
No. 715—

THE NUMBERS GAME

Baseball without statistics? It's hard to imagine. The numerical data that baseball produces seems as vital to the game as bases and the foul lines.

Fans rely on statistics to support their opinions of games and players. Managers and club officials use statistics in evaluating players. Players are as mindful of their batting averages and RBI totals as they are of their salary figures.

Headquarters for the great outpouring of statistics that baseball produces is a suite of small offices in a tall building on West 42nd Street in mid-Manhattan, opposite the New York Public Library. This is the Elias Sports Bureau, presided over by Seymour Siwoff, dean of American sports statisticians. Siwoff's firm also gathers and disseminates statistical data for the National Football League and the National Basketball Association.

The statistics for each baseball game are collected by the official scorer, one of the local baseball writers who covers the home team, and entered by him on a large report form, which is sent to Siwoff's firm. The figures are then checked and entered onto ledger sheets. Tables are prepared and mimeographed each week and sent out to the press, radio, television, and team and league officials.

Each team also has its own statistician. He keeps a pitch-by-pitch account of all games. Rather than figure batting averages, slugging percentages, and

such, the team statistician is more concerned with gathering other data on how players perform. How does a particular batter do against right-handed pitching? Against left-handers? How does he perform at home? On the road? How often does he pull the ball? How does he perform when he's behind in the ball-and-strike count? When he's ahead?

Statistical information of this type can prove extremely valuable. For example, it is generally agreed that a left-handed batter performs better against a right-handed pitcher. But it isn't always the case. A few left-handed hitters do as well against southpaws, or almost as well, as they do when facing right-handers. Information of this type is simple for the statistician to determine.

Television and radio announcers also have their own statisticians. Listeners are often very aware of this fact.

To the average hitter, one statistic is more important than all others—his batting average. It is figured by dividing the number of at-bats into the number of hits, and carrying the result out to three decimal places.

An "at-bat" is an "official" time at bat, that is, an instance in which the player is given an opportunity to get a hit. It is *not* an at-bat should the batter get a base on balls, be hit by a pitch, be awarded first base because of being interfered with by the catcher, execute a successful sacrifice hit, or hit a

Siwoff scans reports from the field.

sacrifice fly.

A "hit" occurs when the batter reaches first base, or any succeeding base, safely without the aid of an error by a fielder. Any single, double, triple, or home run counts as one hit in compiling a batting average.

Here's an example of how a batting average is computed; the figures refer to Ted Williams' at-bats (456) and hits (185) in 1941:

```
            .4057
    456)185.00
        1824
         2600
         2280
          3200
          3192
             8
```

Average: .406

In order to qualify for a league batting championship, a player must come to bat 3.1 times the number of games scheduled by his team. "Coming to bat" is different from "at-bats." It refers to all plate appearances, a term that includes bases on balls, sacrifices, and so on.

Since major league teams have been playing 162-game schedules in recent years, the minimum number of plate appearances required to qualify for a batting title has been 502. Some minor league teams play 140-game schedules, in which case 434 appearances are required.

Runs batted in, a cumulative total which includes home runs as well as the number of runners driven home, is hitting's second-most-important statistic. And to some players, sluggers mostly, "ribbies," as they are called, are the most important

Message board at White Sox Stadium keeps fans posted on Dick Allen's latest statistics.

statistic of all. Yet it is generally agreed that one's RBI total is a less valid barometer of one's hitting skill than the batting average. The RBI total gives no indication of the opportunity to drive in runs. The third and fourth men in the batting order usually lead the team in RBIs, but it's no wonder. When these men come up to bat, there are usually men on base. They have many more opportunities to drive in runs than the man who leads off or the man who bats second in the lineup. A man's RBI total gives no clue as to his efficiency in driving in runs.

Slugging averages are not as highly esteemed as batting averages or RBI totals, yet all record manuals carry them. A slugging average is figured by dividing the number of at-bats a player has into his "total bases."

Total bases is the sum of bases accounted for by all of a player's hits. A single counts as one in figuring total bases, a double as two, a triple as three, and a home run as four.

When figuring a batter's total bases, bear in mind that his "hit" total is invariably a cumulative figure, representing not only singles, but doubles, triples, and home runs as well. This means then that a double is to be counted as only one, a triple as two, and a home run as three. For example, in one recent year, Dick Allen had 156 hits, including 28 doubles, 5 triples, and 37 home runs. This gave him 305 total bases:

Charts, record books, field glasses, electronic calculator, and telephone are part of the equipment used by Bill Kane, statistician for the New York Yankees.

156	(total hits)
28	(one extra base for each double)
10	(two extra bases for each triple)
111	(three extra bases for each home run)
305	

To compute his slugging percentage for that

year, you would have divided his at-bats—506—into 305.

$$506 \overline{)305.0000} \quad .6027$$

3036
1400
1012   Slugging percentage: .603
3880
3542
338

When grading players offensively, some teams also keep track of the following:

Runs-batted-in percentage (found by dividing a player's total number of hits, walks, and sacrifice flies into the total number of runs batted in).

Runs percentage (found by dividing a player's total number of walks, times hit by the pitch, and total hits into the total number of runs).

On-base percentage (found by dividing a player's total number of walks, times hit by the pitch, and total times at bat into the total number of walks, times hit by the pitch, and hits).

Sacrifice percentage (found by dividing a player's total number of sacrifices and official at-bats into the total number of sacrifices).

Strike-out percentage (found by dividing a player's total number of at-bats into the total number of strikeouts).

Base-on-balls percentage (found by dividing a player's total number of plate appearances into the total number of walks).

In determining their own batting averages, players don't rely on team statisticians nor do they consult Seymour Siwoff. They do the figuring themselves. Indeed, some players are more skilled in long division than hitting outside pitches.

"Sure, I watch my batting average," says Johnny Bench. "It tells the tale of your whole season. Not only the batting average, but runs driven in. If you're not hitting for average and not driving in runs, how can you be considered for MVP?"

THE .400 HITTERS

.424—Rogers Hornsby, St. Louis Cardinals, 1924
.422—Napolean Lajoie, Philadelphia Athletics, 1901
.420—Ty Cobb, Detroit Tigers, 1911
.420—George Sisler, St. Louis Browns, 1922
.410—Ty Cobb, Detroit Tigers, 1912
.408—Joe Jackson, Cleveland Indians, 1908
.407—George Sisler, St. Louis Browns, 1920
.406—Ted Williams, Boston Red Sox, 1941
.403—Harry Heilmann, Detroit Tigers, 1923
.401—Rogers Hornsby, St. Louis Cardinals, 1925
.401—Ty Cobb, Detroit Tigers, 1922
.401—Rogers Hornsby, St. Louis Carinals, 1922
.401—Bill Terry, New York Giants, 1930

ALL-TIME HOME RUN RECORDS

Most home runs, lifetime
714—Babe Ruth, New York Yankees
713—Hank Aaron, Atlanta Braves*
660—Willie Mays, New York Mets
552—Frank Robinson, California Angels*
546—Harmon Killebrew, Minnesota Twins*

536—Mickey Mantle, New York Yankees
534—Jimmy Foxx, Boston Red Sox
521—Ted Williams, Boston Red Sox
512—Ernie Banks, Chicago Cubs
512—Eddie Mathews, Milwaukee Braves
* Still active (1974)

Most home runs, season
61—Roger Maris, New York Yankees, 1961
60—Babe Ruth, New York Yankees, 1927
59—Babe Ruth, New York Yankees, 1921
58—Jimmy Foxx, Philadelphia Athletics, 1932
58—Hank Greenberg, Detroit Tigers, 1938
56—Hack Wilson, Chicago Cubs, 1930
54—Ralph Kiner, Pittsburgh Pirates, 1949
54—Mickey Mantle, New York Yankees, 1961
52—Mickey Mantle, New York Yankees, 1956
52—Willie Mays, San Francisco Giants, 1965

Most seasons leading league, home runs
12—Babe Ruth, New York Yankees

Most home runs, bases full, lifetime
23—Lou Gehrig, New York Yankees

Most home runs, bases full, season
5—Ernie Banks, Chicago Cubs, 1955
5—Jim Gentile, Baltimore Orioles, 1961

TRIPLE-CROWN WINNERS
(Batting, Home Runs, and Runs Batted In)

Ty Cobb, Detroit Tigers, 1909
Heinie Zimmerman, Chicago Cubs, 1912
Rogers Hornsby, St. Louis Cardinals, 1922, 1925
Chuck Klein, Philadelphia Phillies, 1933
Jimmy Foxx, Philadelphia Athletics, 1933
Lou Gehrig, New York Yankees, 1934
Joe Medwick, St. Louis Cardinals, 1937
Ted Williams, Boston Red Sox, 1942, 1947
Mickey Mantle, New York Yankees, 1956
Frank Robinson, Baltimore Orioles, 1966
Carl Yastrzemski, Boston Red Sox, 1967

ALL-TIME BATTING RECORDS

Most seasons leading league, batting average
12—Ty Cobb, Detroit Tigers

Highest batting average, lifetime
.367—Ty Cobb, Detroit Tigers

Most seasons, leading league, slugging average
13—Babe Ruth, New York Yankees

Highest slugging average, lifetime
.690—Babe Ruth, New York Yankees

Highest slugging average, season
.847—Babe Ruth, New York Yankees, 1920

Most plate appearances, lifetime
12,713—Ty Cobb, Detroit Tigers

Most at-bats, lifetime
11,429—Ty Cobb, Detroit Tigers

Most runs scored, lifetime
2,244—Ty Cobb, Detroit Tigers

Most runs scored, season
196—Billy Hamilton, Philadelphia Phillies, 1894

Most hits, lifetime
4,191—Ty Cobb, Detroit Tigers

Most hits, season
257—George Sisler, St. Louis Cardinals, 1920

Most consecutive hits
12—Pinky Higgins, Boston Red Sox, 1938
12—Walt Dropo, Detroit Tigers, 1952

Most hits, game
7—Wilbert Robinson, Baltimore Orioles, 1892

Most games, consecutive hits
56—Joe DiMaggio, New York Yankees, 1941

Most one-base hits, lifetime
3,052—Ty Cobb, Detroit Tigers

Most one-base hits, season
202—Willie Keeler, Baltimore Orioles, 1898

Most two-base hits, lifetime
793—Tris Speaker, Cleveland Indians

Most two-base hits, season
67—Earl Webb, Boston Red Sox, 1931

Most three-base hits, lifetime
312—Sam Crawford, Detroit Tigers

Most three-base hits, season
36—John Owen Wilson, Pittsburgh Pirates, 1912

Most seasons leading league, runs batted in
6—Babe Ruth, New York Yankees

Most runs batted in, lifetime
2,209—Babe Ruth, New York Yankees

Most runs batted in, season
190—Hack Wilson, Chicago Cubs, 1930

Most runs batted in, game
12—Jim Bottomley, St. Louis Cardinals, 1924

Most sacrifice hits, lifetime
511—Eddie Collins, Philadelphia Athletics

Most sacrifice hits, season
67—Roy Chapman, Cleveland Indians, 1917

Most bases on balls, lifetime
2,056—Babe Ruth, New York Yankees

Most bases on balls, season
170—Babe Ruth, New York Yankees

Most hit by pitch, lifetime
192—Minnie Minoso, Chicago White Sox

Most hit by pitch, season
50—Ron Hunt, Montreal Expos, 1971

Most strikeouts, lifetime
1,710—Mickey Mantle, New York Yankees

Most strikeouts, season
189—Bobby Bonds, San Francisco Giants, 1970

Most pinch-hit at-bats, lifetime
507—Smokey Burgess, Chicago White Sox

Most pinch-hit at-bats, season
73—Vic Davalillo, St. Louis Cardinals, 1970

Most pinch-hits, lifetime
144—Smokey Burgess, Chicago White Sox

Most pinch-hits, season
24—Dave Philley, Baltimore Orioles, 1961
24—Vic Davalillo, St. Louis Cardinals, 1970

INDEX